I0427717

Common Sense
*Or Who Is That
   Sitting In My Pew?*

By C.J.
Henning

The politics of life interferes with truth

The truth will be known despite the facts

The facts must be revised to reflect a view

And the view can only be a shadow of reality.

By this shall all men know that history

Is the enemy of repetition.

CHAPTER ONE
Future of the Church

What is our life, but a faint breeze barely felt and soon forgotten? A grain of salt that time savors for a moment then yearns to taste another. What great event brings out our significance to those around us? Why is it so important to impress those who are trying to impress you and are unable to get your attention? Yet, God sees you and takes notes. Our life, each life is not insignificant to our Lord, but we beat ourselves up when we feel we have measured up to the likes of the Apostle Paul, Martin Luther, John Calvin and Billy Graham. Not all are leaders; many are followers who do the hard work anonymously to everyone, but God.

We need to understand that faith has no fifteen minutes of fame. Actually it is an eternal life of spiritual fame. Faith brings work that seems to be thankless and sometimes without immediate results. Perhaps the Lord will tell us after we enter Heaven the impact, or lack thereof, we had on the lives of others. It is better that we do not know until then for it would puff us up to the point of uselessness to the Spirit that lives within us.

We have a need to be recognized, a yearning to be self-sufficient and a yen to have a purpose. However, to be recognized might only bring danger, ridicule or just curiosity. To be self-sufficient means the need to persevere and protect those things that have made us that way depending on our need to appreciate our purpose, to applaud our attempts to be meaningful and to pat ourselves on the back for the greatness we bring to this life. If this is your yearning, it is not the Lord's for your future:

"If the world hates you, keep in mind that it hated me first. If you belonged to the world it would love you as its own. As it is, you do belong to the world, but I have chosen you out of the world."

John 15: 18,19

When you kneel before God, all eternity recognizes your decision. Self-sufficiency is not part of the Lord's agenda for reliance on His blessings brings sufficiency for the self.

To have personal purpose only interferes with the purpose of God. We may never fulfill our dreams and goals, but it is the purpose of God to fulfill His goals through you and with those goals your dreams are fulfilled. The only difference is that the fulfillment of those dreams may be completely different from what you first wanted. You will realize by following the Lord that those voices shouting all around you are words of desperation and frustration.

We have been informed that in order for the church to survive the 21st Century and it must change with the society in which it lives. First, the church accepted women as pastors and priests. There was a minor tremor, but it survived. Now practicing homosexuals are given the privilege of being pastors and even bishops within the church. Should we welcome this as another step to tolerance and acceptance of all men? Is this the future of the true church which will encourage society to embrace Christianity? Bishop Robinson said it best: "Homosexuality is a special gift from God." Huh? What? This heretical comment has been accepted by the Episcopal Church to show acceptance and tolerance of all men. Is this the future of the church?

Is the goal of every church to be successful only to balance budgets and fill the pews however possible. In accepting all walks of life and lifestyles does it show a growing maturity that will honor God in His ever changing openness to the new faith. Is this the new theme that Christians want? I do not think that anyone who has read the

Bible would remotely accept this kind of "new church"

We are told that Churches are a place of worship not politics or issues of national importance such as abortion, pornography, euthanasia, taxes or any controversy. We are told the church is not an institution to cause grief for the government or those parts of society who believe the opposite of what the church teaches. The courts say they can decide the measure of moral and

ethical values better then the church. The court says this is why we have Separation of Church and State to protect all Americans from the abuse that Christianity has been known to cause for its entire history.

The liberal interpretation of how the church must be a place for scripture reading except those parts that incite vicious debate over the above moral questions. According to the liberal cause the church should not have its hand in government, courtrooms, schools, media or theater. The Supreme Court has stated that there is to be a Separation between Church and State so that even the mention of Jesus the Christ constitutes grounds for dismissal of teachers in schools and sends a red flag up for those seeking public office.

School prayer is banned to keep faith out of the classroom. Moral and ethical behavior is now taught by those who have multiple exceptions to any and all rules of proper decorum. The new definition of life everlasting involves cryogenics and scientific research. The road to heaven is a wide road open to Buddhists, Muslims, Atheists, Republicans and Democrats because it wouldn't be fair to exclude anyone. It is not right according to liberals that God decides who will go and who won't. He must be trivialized into an Elysian Fields mythical creature in the guise of Paganism and Secularism which cannot expect a heavenly life for living a good life.

With liberals and atheists there is no heaven or hell in actuality they are a perception of a great place and a horrible place to keep the masses in check. Heaven is in the mind of the beholder such as Muslims dying in Jihad that allows an afterlife with 40 or more virgins, for atheists it is complete silence and oblivion while for Christians it is singing forever before the throne of God. With many if there is a hell it is where you pass gas in a vacuum with no place to go and you stink up the place forever. Hell might be full of flames without air conditioning or it could be an endless pit where you are free falling forever. Needless to say by these naysayers that no such places exist so we hope for the best in our short time on earth.

The Democratic platform has decided, though they reversed it, that God has no place in their party. They also wanted to ignore Jerusalem and not defend Israel. They are telling us that they will make this nation in their image and not God's. No one not even God can tell us what to do. Do you see a pattern here? The platform says we will kill as many children through abortion as we want. We will tax into oblivion all who live well. Socialism is a good thing though it leads to abject poverty for all. We will change the Bible so it is benign and not harmful to society. We do not want to suffer guilt for anything. We want entitlements for all so just print more money though it leads to financial destruction. Israel is not our concern. Muslim law is not so bad. Terrorists are just freedom fighters. Christians are just uptight amoral Victorians living in the wrong century. Political Correctness is not meant to destroy freedom of religion, speech or press. According to liberals the purpose of Political Correctness is to divide and conquer any society, to make individuals change their moral compass and stifle free speech that questions a socialist future.

Those who don't believe think there is so little time to correct the damage that the Will of God has brought. They believe if He did exist it would be better to adjust His thinking more to our liking than accept the vision of the past. To do this we must change scripture so that it is not politically incorrect and be reinterpreted as the new (The Voice) Bible that has just recently been written. Now angels are messengers, Jesus is 'The Voice', Christ is "The Anointed One" and scripture is a TV sitcom.

Now more arguments against the church from the media starts with how any church can promote moral and ethical behavior when thousands of children have been molested. If it happened within the Catholic Church does it not stand to reason that all Christian faiths are guilty, too? Gay ministers in the Methodist Church and gay Bishops in the Episcopal Church give conflicting views and feelings within their own congregations. Scriptural ignorance is rampant in our society which is why the church must commit in one voice a change so that all churches become unified. Now we are into an ecumenical challenge using a radical voice that does not conflict with a global society. We hear that the church must come into the 21st Century and not sit in the 1st Century. We are told that nothing in the past can bring us together because the past can only tear us apart. Is not all this what we are hearing in the media every day? Is this not the garbage in and garbage out our parents warned us about.

Historically, the church has kept the moral sense in schools and government without handing out condoms and explaining sexual positions. You cannot teach the moral and ethical values without the sense that God is watching over your shoulders. The view that God watches and judges you every minute of the day was a staple of the church for thousands of years. However, the law can be circumvented by reinterpretation to give freedom to those who corrupt life and break the law. Since God cannot be circumvented He must be relegated to stand before the Supreme Court.

We can thank our founders, most of whom were Christians, for the break with England to start a new nation, under God, that became the most successful nation in history. We can condemn those who defy God and allow our country to suffer under $120 trillion in debt. How we can allow this to continue is beyond the scope of any common sense.

CHAPTER TWO
Politics of Religion
Excluding Religion

Political correctness is the perverse enjoyment of seeing others suffer under a rule of law that has no meaning other than the subtle innocuous perverseness to taunt the will of God. Knowing it is wrong only enhances the need to force others to believe it is politically correct to accept the moral consequences concerning the immorality of the sin.

To confuse ourselves more we must pass laws that make us believe that the sky is falling and God has crashed into the sea causing another religious tsunami. Having done so, He is seen by many as the Supreme Charlatan we all knew He had been. That statement becomes politically correct in the insane world of social madness and relative to the lies of socio-political expediency.

The reference of Separation of Church and State is from a letter by Thomas Jefferson in 1802 and it was not a legal binding testament, but an opportunistic excuse to attack Christianity. It is why the Russian Constitution put it in writing because Christianity is to be feared for it opens the door to a wealth of individual freedom. Communism cannot survive in a free state or a Christian state.

Looking at it a different way maybe we should have separation of Church and State for some obvious reasons. The Church teaches that you should not kill, steal, or commit adultery. The State teaches that killing unborn children is all right, stealing from government coffers is acceptable when asking for higher taxes while passing pork legislation and approval ratings rise for those politicians who are adulterous with criminal records, but only with the Democratic Party.

The Church teaches that the Bible is a good thing, but the State teaches that the Bible is a bad thing for public schools, government events, and if possible, churches because the Bible is the cause of bigotry, intolerance, and war. The Church teaches moral backbone while the State punishes moral back bone.

Yes, Church and State is incompatible and perhaps we should keep them separate. It is unlikely that there will be a truce in the near future for we are in the last days and this last bastion of freedom must fall if our Lord is to come again. Sadly, for the prophecy of Revelation to be fulfilled all things must pass and the Antichrist must rise up.

"And the dragon stood on the shore of the sea. And I saw a beast coming out of the sea. He had ten horns and seven heads, with ten crowns on his horns, and on each head a blasphemous name.

The beast I saw resembled a leopard, but had feet like those of a bear and a mouth like that of a lion. The dragon gave the beast his power and great authority. One had a fatal wound, but the fatal wound had been healed. The whole world was astonished and followed the beast, and they also worshipped the beast and asked

'Who is like the beast? Who can make war against him?'

The beast was given a mouth to utter proud words and blasphemies and to exercise his authority for forty-two months.

He opened his mouth to blaspheme God, and to slander His name and His dwelling place and those who live in heaven. He was given power to make war against the saints and conquer them. He was given authority over every tribe, people, language, and nation.

All inhabitants of the earth will worship the beast-all whose names have not been written in the book of life belonging to the Lamb that was slain from the creation of the world."

Revelation 13: 1-8

We prefer not to see where the future is going for everyone in the world. We prefer to sit and watch thinking it is a new series on the Sci-Fi channel. We are waiting for the superhero to come at the last minute and save us. That superhero is Jesus, but it comes with a price. We want free intervention without our involvement which is why our laziness will bring us to the feet of the Antichrist. It is archaic to talk about what we read in the Bible. We think we are more civilized where the myths of God and man do not coincide with the New Age. Yet the New Age encompasses horoscopes, witchcraft, crystals, she-male gods, mysticism, spiritual narcissism and good luck charms. We have not changed from the age of Jesus only have become more refined in hiding our sins and more sophisticated in dishonoring God.

Showing right from wrong is only an ambiguity in recent literature and theater. Tolerance for all things is acceptable in everything except the Bible. The Bible is considered an antiquated morality play signifying nothing. Christianity is not subject for serious discussion except by those less enlightened....behind closed doors....in a closet....with bags over their heads. However, the discussion must be managed and directed with the thought that

God is a myth, a frightening image like a bully in a schoolyard or a boogeyman in the shadows watching your every move. It is far from the truth.

"If My people, who are called by My name, will humble themselves and pray and seek My face and turn from

their wicked ways, then I will forgive their sins and heal their land"

II Chronicles 7:14

What future do atheists, hedonists, and anarchists offer but chaos. We already see it in our government, schools, and public life. There is even confusion in the church to stand for a righteous life. If the Ten Commandments offer common sense why is it forced from public view? If we accept the premise of these words why do we openly do those things which were once secret, hidden, and ungodly? How do we justify a democracy that shakes its fist at God? We cannot justify it because we are a Republic not a democracy. A Republic is based on Judeo-Christian law that are superior to democratic law. In a democracy the people can vote that murder is not a crime thereby bypassing the moral law of God. Only a moral people can keep our freedoms. An immoral people have no use for them.

Back to separation of Church and State. Without it children would bring Bibles to school instead of guns, politicians would be impelled to tell the truth and actually represent those who voted them in, and yes, marriage would be between a man and a woman with politer children. However we are told that living a godly life would spoil the economy, ruin selfish degradation and offer no future to the hopelessly rich. We would have lower taxes because brother would help brother without crying out for government assistance. Crime might even be lowered because we would again have a social conscious. Yes, the church is too much of a destructive force as well as the media tells us.

Much of the problems we have today are government representatives who have been in power too long thinking they can do whatever they please and still be re-elected. Our own citizens reward murderers, adulterers, homosexuals and felons with a free pass to run our government yet wonder why we are in such a social mess. The government we have in place represents the sorry state of our national affairs. How can we have honest government if we are not honest ourselves?

Where is the Church in all this? Well, listen. Do you hear anything? Me either.

When the sleeping giant of our faith wakes up it may be too late.

Already Roman Catholics and Protestant members are turning to Islam because the Christian Church offers little obedience to spiritual needs of those looking for moral direction. The Wiccans are growing because they

give tangible ways to touch the spirit even though it is in magic and nature. The Transcendental faiths help those who are in need through physical options and meditation.

The needs and wants of our society are both physical and spiritual. We need to be touched in both ways through our Church. Many of us feel isolated in pews sitting next to nameless faces that quickly disperse to their cars and homes. The Christian Church is no longer offering spiritual meat in their pulpits, but excuses and politically correct pabulum. We are the salt of the earth not the skim milk diluting the horrors of this world.

We are under attack because we are not of the right faith. Soon we will not be the stronger faith. I have read the Koran and there is no mercy, salvation or hope within its covers. Those who do not agree with the Koran's teachings and follow its principles must be enslaved or put to death.

"Verily the worst cattle in the sight of God are those who are obstinate infidels and will not believe. ....and think not that the unbelievers have escaped God's vengeance, for they shall not weaken the power of God. Therefore prepare against them what force ye are able and troops of horse whereby ye may strike a terror into the enemy of God and your enemy and into other infidels besides them."

Al Koran
translated by George Sale 1880

There is no peace within its covers until the whole world is converted by the sword or punished with slavery by those who consider themselves masters of that faith. Women are meaningless except as chattel for brothels, slavery to their husbands and even prostitutes in heaven. They proudly speak of 42 virgins at the disposal of those who are suicide bombers.

"It shall not be lawful for thee to take other women to wife hereafter, nor to exchange any of thy wives for them, although their beauty please thee; except thy slaves whom thy right hand shall possess and God observeth all things."

Al Koran
translated by George Sale 1880

If this was a religion confined to its own boundaries there would no problem from the rest of the world. However, it is a religion that wants to force everyone to live as they do. This is where the great divide begins. With Christianity you have a choice to accept Christ or reject Him without the sword. With Islam it is believe or face the sword.

What does the Bible say about husband and wife? Ephesians 5:25-29:

"Husbands, love your wives, just as Christ loved the church
and gave Himself up for her to make her holy, cleansing her
by the washing with water through the word, and to present
her to Himself as a radiant church, without stain or wrinkle
or any other blemish, but holy and blameless. In this same way husbands ought to love their wives as their own bodies.
He who loves his wife loves himself. After all, no one ever hated his own body, but he feeds and cares for it, just as Christ
cares for the church.'"

What is life but a futile race with death? The dust from the race left behind is us. What is our soul but a joyful gift to God?

The freedoms we enjoy are because our forefathers believed, not in themselves alone, but in God as inspiration should be a joyful noise to God. Do we not believe what we tell other nations about the largess and bounty of our land comes from our faithfulness to God? Why do we yearn to destroy the Eden we created for a hell that fulfills nothing in the human spirit?

The fascination of Political Correctness is the fractured mirror of egotistical comparison. We want everyone to be as we think they should be not as we are. We express moral relativism only as a teaching tool for others, not ourselves. The Church is being deceived in the guise of political correctness that searches for the perfect New Testament condemning no one, Churches without sinners looking for the next Billy Graham, tax code numbers and waiting for God Himself to stand in our midst saying "Can you hear Me now?"

To the public outcry that the Cross in city squares, in front of government buildings, on state flags and even pinned on lapels offends you; that the Christian message is offensive to be heard; that the audacity of our forefathers to burden us with Christian moral obligations and that the Word of God has no place in society; what do you offer that gives hope, freedom, salvation and peace?

What other faith gives you the right to choose what you believe without a sword to your throat? Other religions offer no belief in God, but reincarnation of endless lives and endless despair. What religion do we replace Christianity with that guarantees freedom of speech, freedom of press and yes, freedom of those religions who curse us? Christianity has a great tolerance of those who abuse those freedoms. It is the sin we abhor as does God, but everyone has the choice to throw away their lives or save them.

The Bible is the blueprint of freedom for freedom, the Cross the symbol of redemption not historical hypocrisy and the empty tomb the promise of eternal life. If that is not so, show me something better.

It is easier to use moral tweezers to pick out the small thorns in your side. The difficulty lies in the spear, sword and stake impaling our sides making our tweezers more difficult to use.

"Why do you look at the speck of sawdust in your brother's
                    eye and pay no
attention to the plank in your own eye? How

can you say to your brother, 'Let me take the speck out of your eye,' when all the time there is a plank in your own eye?

You hypocrite, first take the plank out of your own eye, and then you will see clearly to remove the speck out of your brother's eye."

Matthew 7: 3-5

It is not easy to be what Christ wants us to be and still be ourselves. Is it Christ's will to be abrupt and forceful in your faith? Should we be weeping sheep so others come to Christ out of pity? Should we be silent so we do not have to defend our belief and just hope they see Christ in us? Such confusion, such mediocrity, such indecision is not part of us.

We should not offend by insisting on conversion, yet, perhaps, insisting on an answer. We should not point out the deficiencies of those who we wish to convert, but we bare witness to our conversion through the old deficiencies for which Christ forgave us. Our deficiencies can be our strength for witnessing to those who might understand the imperfections and realize they can have hope, too.

Our wealth is spiritual, our power is from God, our happiness is in Christ's assurance of eternal life and our hope lies in the peace that the Bible gives us. What can hold us here if Christ awaits us? What holds us is the purpose of not coming to Christ alone, but with others who walk side by side next to us to the gates of heaven.

There are some of us who have always known God existed, but were afraid to acknowledge Him. Is it because we believed we would not have a chance to enjoy our life by such a commitment? Doesn't God hinder us in enjoying the better things in life? Sex? Wealth? Power?

Each one must be addressed to show that they have a different and better meaning to God. The first is the most desirable and fulfilling in our natural needs which is sexual desire. Sexual desire is a force stronger than any other that makes us do things which we would not normally accept if we were fulfilled in a relationship. Marriage controls urges that would otherwise cause dysfunctional choices in work, in social surroundings, educational choices and the like.

"'Everything is permissible for me'- but not everything
            is beneficial. 'Everything is permissible for me.' –but I will
            not be mastered by anything. 'Food for the stomach and

the stomach for food' – but God will destroy them both.

The body is not meant for sexual immorality, but for the Lord, and the Lord for the body."

I Corinthians 6: 12-13

Indiscriminate sex leaves an emotional void that's never filled and the possibility of health problems to all involved. It is an orgasmic wasteland. Sexual desire in marriage fills the void in the needs of release, love, companionship, friendship and bonding. One night stands cannot do this nor can living together bring confidence in the relationship. The realization that one or the other can leave without notice can never bring peace in any relationship. When things become difficult there is no reason to stay and work out the problems. Marriage is not perfect, but it is the greatest contract in the world where negotiations can be settled with a kiss and hard times with an embrace and prayer.

The second is wealth which when used in God's plan is an honor when earned honestly, but considered ultimately useless to uphold the spirit. Wealth in God's plan is meeting basic needs for your family and giving to the Lord that part which He has given you to meet your needs. Wealth is a difficult balance between greed and comfort. One would have to choose ultimately between God and the riches of this earth.

"Now a man came up to Jesus and asked, 'Teacher, what
good thing must I do to get eternal life?'
'Why do you ask me about what is good?' Jesus replied.
'There is only One who is good. If you want to enter life,
Obey the commandments.'
'Which ones?' the man inquired.
Jesus replied, 'Do not murder, do not commit adultery, do not steal, do not give false testimony, honor your father and
mother, and love your neighbor as yourself.
'All these I have kept,' the young man said. 'What do I still lack? Jesus said 'If you want to be perfect, go, sell your
possessions and give to the poor, and you will have treasure in heaven. Then come, follow me.'
When the young man heard this, he went away sad, because he had great wealth.
Then Jesus said to his disciples, 'I tell you the truth, it is hard for a rich man to enter the kingdom of heaven. Again I
you, it is easier for a camel to go through the

eye of a needle than a rich man to enter the kingdom of heaven"

Matthew 19: 16-23

This is not to say being rich is unchristian, but the ability to freely let go of your wealth for the sake of Christ is the point. Jesus does not condemn wealth, but the attitude that riches can take His place in your life is the heart of the matter. If you care more about your wealth, then the Lord your God will fade to the background making it impossible to enter the kingdom of God.

Power is third and most dangerous because it comes in many forms. It could be control over family and friends. It could be power over a whole community. It could be power over governments. Power corrupts completely if God does not put you there and you believe the power that you have was not from God.

"My message and my preaching were not with wise and

persuasive words, but with a demonstration of the

Spirit's power, so that your faith might not rest on men's

wisdom, but God's power. We do, however, speak a

message of wisdom among the
mature, but not the
wisdom of this age or of the rulers of
this age, who are coming to nothing."
I Corinthians 2: 4-6

In the corruptibility of men and
women things happen that are
incomprehensible and we ask "Why me
Lord?" His answer seems to be "Why not?"
Why would He say such a thing? Is it
because we are unfaithful? Lack the will to
understand? Do we not see the big picture?
Isn't there an easy outline that can present
itself, a How-to book or some great scholar
to explain the mess we put ourselves in? Are
we not smart enough to extricate ourselves
through logic the troubles we face? Can we
not convince God that we have the best
perspective on life and know more of both
physical and spiritual things?

"The Spirit searches all things, even
the deep things of
God. For who among men knows the
thoughts of a man
except the man's spirit within him? In
the same way no
one knows the thoughts of God except
the Spirit of God.

We have not received the spirit of the world but the Spirit who is from God, that we may understand what what God has freely given us. This is what we speak, not in words taught us by human wisdom but in words taught by the Spirit, expressing spiritual truths in spiritual words. The man without the spirit does not accept the things that come from the Spirit of God, for they are foolishness to him, and he cannot understand them, because they are spiritually discerned. The spiritual man makes judgments about all things, but he himself is not subject to any man's judgment:

'For who has known the mind of the Lord
That he may instruct Him?'
But we have the mind of Christ."
I Corinthians 10-16

I will answer the "Why me Lord?' with a personal footnote. I have diabetes, high blood pressure, Diverticulitis, Rheumatic heart, Arthritis in both knees and lower back, high cholesterol, enlarged prostate, recently had cancer surgery and scars from childhood coming from acne and boils. I consider myself a walking pestilence at times, but the favor of the Lord has been that I can use the thorns in my side as a testimony for Christ.

Not enough? Tragedy must be part of my life, too? In 2004 over Thanksgiving my mother was stabbed to death and my older brother brought down by a shotgun. Stranger did it? No, my younger brother now in prison whom I still write to and pray for his salvation. The reason for the killing? Over money, an inheritance.

I grew up with family surrounded with relations involving attempted suicides, alcoholism, manic depression, bigotry, paranoia, pornographic addiction, greed, hate, and physical abuse. How in the world did the Lord

find me out of that morass of chaos? Why would I think there was any hope for me? With all the self-destruction why would I believe God exists? Televangelists have fallen from mighty religious perches so why would I follow Christ?

"Then Jesus declared: 'I am the bread of life. He who comes

To me will never be hungry, and he who believes in me

will never be thirsty. But as I told you, you have seen me and

still you do not believe. All that the Father gives me will come to me, and whoever comes to me I will never drive away. For

I have come down from heaven not to do my will but to do the

will of Him who sent me. And this is the will of Him who sent

me, that I shall lose none of all that He has given me, but raise

them up at the last day. For my Father's will is that everyone

who looks to the Son, and believes in him shall have eternal

life. And I will raise him up at the last day."

John 6:35-40

I was personally rejected in my youth by family, church and my school. Why would I forgive the torment I endured most of my teenage life? Why would I care about them? Why did I have to suffer so much if it seems I gained so little?

"Therefore, since we have been justified through faith,

we have peace with God through our Lord Jesus Christ,

through whom we have gained access by faith into

his grace in which we now stand. And we rejoice

in the hope of the glory of God. Not only so, but we

also rejoice in our sufferings, because we know that

suffering produces perseverance, character; and

hope. And hope does not disappoint us, because God

has poured out His love into our hearts by the Holy Spirit,

whom He has given us."

Romans 5:1-5

I always knew God existed, but I did not want to come to Him. I wanted to be left alone and he refused to stop calling me to come home. I wept, I shook my fist, but I wanted the comfort and the embrace of Christ that I believed I did not deserve. I fought every day until he lifted me up and took the pain away. I could not forgive myself and he said I had to.

Chapter Three

I pledge allegiance to the first thing that comes my way

There is a political battle over the Pledge of Allegiance and the Ten Commandments over a few words and what the other symbolizes. First let us look at the Pledge of Allegiance and what the words imply:

"I pledge allegiance to the flag" and pledging allegiance we acknowledge and accept basic freedoms with their responsibilities that our flag represents. It counters against the 'One World Order' and favors patriotism in body and deed. My opinion of the flag is the red stripe the bloody stain of those who died for our freedoms so we can live in peace and follow the faith we choose. The white stripe represents the guiding light to those who are oppressed to come to our country. The blue background is for each man and woman to feel like royalty, to become whatever their talents and abilities will allow them to become. The stars are not only symbols of our states, but the far reaching goals that a free people can strive for and achieve if they work for it.

"And to the United States of America" is a second pledge to a united country in war and peace. We are a country that promises unity through diversity and the hope of equal rights for all. It is a country of a common language not a nation speaking in tongues without interpretation or understanding.

"And to the Republic for which it stands" which is a country that stands against oppression and for life, liberty, and the pursuit of happiness. The right to succeed with the gifts God, yes, God, has given us and the individuality that who you are matters as much as what you are. That who you are can be a pillar for societal truths.

"One nation" not hyphenated, not gender-fractured, not politically intolerant, nor religiously ambiguous or capitalistically restricted. We should be one nation looking forward to the future and holding hands with the past where all men are free to be their best. We need to be one nation with the resolve to stay free ignoring the clamor of those who yearn for socialism, who ignore the tragedies of history and wish to repeat it or those who divide us with words of impending doom.

"Under God" which does not mean Buddha, Satan, Kalee, or any other stone monument that is as cold as the rock from which it was made is thrust upon us by derelict souls. Under Him who made us, who guides us, who protects us and blesses us, we do acknowledge His presence in this land. God, as presented in Scripture, not in the media, is our hope and salvation that will keep this country free.

"Indivisible" not divided, so strong that no hammer, no sword, no lines of division can fracture the strength and unity of our nation. A solid wall for the world to see that we will stand and fight for our right to be free must not have cracks or signs of weakness that will give our enemies a foothold on our shores.

"With liberty and justice for all" which means all, no exceptions for anyone, no matter the political correctness or cries of injustice for the wrong reasons or how famous he or she might be in the dispensation of that justice. We can sit and reason what the meaning of is, is, but it must not confuse the wheels of truth.

Perhaps you do not agree with the definitions. Maybe we need an alternative Pledge for those who disagree with what the original represents? Then I offer this for the politically correct crowd:

"I pledge allegiance to myself" for it is myself that I am interested in and no one else. Who else can decide on my happiness and instant personal gratification, but myself? I am the most important human being on the face of the earth and why should I not be satisfied and be fulfilled before anyone else?

"But not to the United States of America and no one else in particular" for this country only gets in the way of my self-indulgence. If I pledge allegiance to the United States of America then I have to leave myself behind and think of someone else. Let someone else honor, cherish and give their life to this country, not me. Heck, I may have to do it myself and that would be unthinkable. And why should I bother with anyone else unless it leads to my own self-satisfaction and gratification?

"And to the Republic for which I have no stand" for I need to know what is politically correct at the time I make any stand. However, sitting on the fence can afford me the best view which side to jump down on in time of trouble. Who knows where the power will come from and how long we will be a republic? I can not possibly chance making the wrong decision.

"One hyphenated nation" for we are not all Americans but Afro-Americans, Latin-Americans, Native-Americans, Asian-Americans or illegal-Americans. There are no true Americans who stand together in times of need, in times of war or in times of disaster. If someone is overlooked it is because of some hyphenated reason. Each of our hyphenated countrymen can never be right for we have our own agenda which none of us can agree upon. We must stay hyphenated to keep our security, our identity so that we are not swallowed up by Nationalism or Patriotism.

"Under no God" for I do not believe He has ever existed and what right does He have in interfering with my life? God belongs in a closet for those idiots who think some ethereal being can be trusted in overseeing our affairs and those of our country. Besides, what god is approved to oversee this country? Before we accept "Under God" we must identify, approve and vote who this non-American ethereal being is before we accept that same being to help rule our nation. So far He has only divided us.

"Divided" for we need to be divided or how else can we show opposition to those things we disagree on? We need to be divided to keep our nation off balance so we will know we aren't manipulated by the Far Right or the Far Left. Division is good. Division is a divine right though God does not exist as long as the divinity is man and not a spiritual mist.

"With liberty and justice for those who can afford it" for it is necessary to have the ways and means to get out of any criminal behavior which is the American way. If you can't afford to defend yourself then it is your fault for being the loser that you are and you deserve to go to jail. This way the rest of us can enjoy the good life and the pursuit of happiness as we see fit.

Is this not the way we look at things in a society without God? Do we not shake our fists at the heavens and yell to God "Leave us alone!"?

"With the tongue we praise our Lord and Father, and

With it we curse men, who have been made in God's

likeness. Out of the same mouth come praise and cursing.

My brothers, this should not be. Can both fresh water

and salt water flow from the same spring? My brothers,

can a fig tree bear olives, or a grapevine bear figs? Neither

can a salt spring produce fresh water?"

James 3: 9-12

Why would we change things only to make it incongruous to the nature of God and His teachings? If we do not like the truth do we just change the wording to uphold our sins instead of grieving over them? If we change the Ten Commandments to be less objectionable, do we serve God's purpose? Perhaps the following suggestion would be more acceptable:

1) We will have no gods before us.
2) You shall bow down to no god and make no image unless other images are constructed to make it fair and competitive for all other gods. No god shall be left behind.
3) You shall not curse anyone in the name of any god for it will be considered a hate crime.
4) Remember Sunday only as the laws in your state allows any business to be open. You will work seven days as needed as Sunday is like any other day. It is the Lord's own fault He rested on the seventh day for imagine all the things He could have created. That is, if God created this mess in the first place.
5) Honor your father and mother, stepfather and stepmother, mother and mother, father and father, single mom, single dad, and the psychiatrist who helps you

understand why you have no personal vested interest in family.

6) You shall not murder, except for a just cause such as war, abortion, euthanasia, or an intruder found unwelcome in your home. If accosted outside, make sure you bring the intruder inside the house to cover all the bases in this commandment.

7) You shall not commit adultery depending on the definition of adultery or you get caught in mid-adultery.

8) You shall not steal except in certain circumstances which are reviewable such as if your family were starving and weighed less than half your original body weight or you are a CEO in a major company trying to improve your shareholders assets.

9) You shall not give false testimony unless you are running for political office, trying to keep political office, can find two witnesses to testify on your behalf and/or you know what the definition of is, is.

10) You shall not covet your neighbor's wife, his house, or anything that is your neighbor's. However, you can force him out by sending obscene mail to his boss with the neighbor's return e-mail, set fire to his car, and leave love notes to him under the door for his wife to find. When he loses his job, his wife divorces him

and he sells the house, you can purchase the house and console his wife. This way you no longer covet the house, but own it. You do not covet his wife for now you have married her.

Our freedoms disappear every day beginning with the Freedom of Speech where political correctness dictates our strength, language and possessions. Hate language is an accusation used against those who speak about issues such as abortion, euthanasia and moral decay. Religious barriers filled with barbed wire that keep God and Christ out of schools deny our heritage. We can not speak against these things if we are ruled by liberal bigots and intolerant right wingers. Does not God speak against these things, too? Is God a bigot, a homophobe or an intolerant right winger? He must be if He has already ruled that such people who support these things will never enter heaven.

"Do you not know that the wicked will not inherit the
    kingdom of God? Do not be deceived; Neither the sexually
        immoral nor idolaters nor male prostitutes nor homosexual

offenders nor thieves not the greedy nor drunkards nor
    slanderers nor swindlers will inherit the kingdom of God."

I Corinthians 6: 9,10

"He said to me: 'It is done. I am the Alpha and Omega, the
    Beginning and the End. To him who is thirsty I will give to
    drink without cost from the spring of the water of life. He who
    overcomes will inherit all this, and I will be his God and he will
    be my son. But the cowardly, the unbelieving, the vile, the
    murderers, the sexually immoral, those who practice the magic
    arts, the idolaters, and all liars-their place will be in the fiery
    lake of burning sulfur. This is the second death."

Revelation 21: 6-8

Too harsh? Perhaps, the last two passages weren't clear enough with its bigoted right wing language. How long will we as Christians be silent while our country and the rest of the world excuse themselves from God's wrath and His grace?

Freedom of the press is only a freedom within a small group of individuals who dictate what we read and what truth might be available for that particular day. No longer are there two sides to a question, but not even a question. Do you think for one minute that a non-democratic society would tolerate even a hint of truth? Do you think those trying to take away our freedoms will allow the press to do whatever it wants? When can the deafening sounds of silence ever weigh in on those who corrupt the Bill of Rights?

We are concerned, as well we should, about terrorism against our country. Unfortunately, we have an enemy within our borders. So we must ask ourselves when it was a crime to seek the appointment of a Christian to the Supreme Court? When was it a danger to our society to be elected President because of his faith in God? How is it only non-Christians can govern this country which was ironically founded by Christians?

Jesus the Christ and God are not swear words. Despite common ignorance it is not best to turn your back on God. He will have the last word. If you believe only dust to dust why bother to work within the confines of society? Why not do what you want if nothing matters? Nothing can stop you from enjoying life as you see fit no matter who you step on, who you destroy in business or how many times you use men and women as you like?

What reason would you worry? Take life as it comes because sex is the breakfast of champions no matter whose bed you are lying on. Lunacy rules!

"And I'll say to myself: 'You have plenty of good
    things laid up for many years. Take life easy; eat
    drink and be merry.'"
Luke 12: 19

If God is dead wear the pin proudly and go to your grave with a smile on your face. Why not? If there is nothing beyond the grave, what stops you? If God be dead what is there to fear?

"If there is no God
What void do we live in?
If there is no God
What purpose is there in life?
If there is no God
Our minds are just mazes within a puzzle.
If there is no God
The death of believers is pointless.

If there is no God
Then Hell is everywhere.
If there is no God
Death is a cataclysmic abyss.
If there is no God
Right and wrong are mere
perceptions.
If there is no God
Joy, laughter, forgiveness are
delusions.
If there is no God."

C. J. Henning

Why do you keep looking over your shoulder? Oblivion is, also, a sense of ethereal numbness. There is nothing to remember, to regret, nothing to be nourished or rewarded. Since God is not God, the darkness can be inviting after a life of deafening pleasure and self-emulation. Just because you have psoriasis of the soul don't think the itching will stop after death. Your hope is that there is no more scratching at the moral rash of society, no more bed sores of Christian morals and beliefs nipping at your skin. Who cares?

"The fool in his heart says, 'There is no God.'
They are corrupt, their deeds are vile;
There is no one who does good......

All have turned aside,
They have together become corrupt;
There is no one who does good,
Not even one."

Psalm 14: 1,3

CHAPTER FOUR

*Excerpts From First Confusion
of The Book
Socialiticus Liberalitis : The Beatitudes*

Blessed are the poor in spirit
For they will always vote Democratic
Blessed are those who mourn
For they will protest against any war.
Blessed are the meek
For they can be manipulated.
Blessed are those who hunger
For they are the good sound bytes.
Blessed are those who are merciful
For they can be deceived.
Blessed are the pure in heart
For they will never invest in
Hollywood.
Blessed are the peacemakers
For they will march on Washington.
Blessed are those who are persecuted
For they keep the ACLU in business
Where Christians need not apply.
Blessed are you when people insult
you, persecute you and falsely say all kinds
of evil against you for Christ's sake, for it
tells us that the news media has done its job.
You may be the salt of the earth, but
we are the sweetener to sugarcoat the
bitterness of life.

Be careful to do your acts of giving, caring and uplifting before cameras and the media, for acts of kindness without media attention is wasted coverage.

And when you pray, pray to angels, ethereal beings, the Great Void or the Supreme Consciousness. If you do not do these things you will be considered a right wing, politically incorrect deluded individual that will never add a cent to the DNC.

You have heard that you do not break your oath

For that is what the courts are for.

You have heard it said an eye for an eye and a tooth for a tooth

And we agree with this form of philosophy.

You have heard that it was said to love your neighbor

But we say first check their portfolio, medical records, views on euthanasia, abortion, taxes, Republicans and right wing Christians to see if they merit your love.

It has been said that anyone who divorces his wife must give her a document of divorce.

So, give it to her plus the house and bank accounts. She'll give you the dog. A fair trade.

We are the light of the world if you cannot see us or hear us on cable, change the light bulb.

Do not think we have come to abolish the law, but to add to them many more laws and sub-laws that it will be impossible for you not to break them.

You have heard it said not to commit murder, but we have made an addendum that murder does not include abortion, euthanasia or the death penalty.

You have heard that was said to the people not to commit adultery, but if your wife commits adultery go out and do likewise. The act of adultery cannot be attached to prurient magazines or on-line pornography even though physical contact is fantasized.

Finally, why look for the dust in your brother's eyes when you can find the beam in your politicians and religious leaders? How can you say "Let's take the dust out of your eye!"when it is easier to point out the defect to those around you? Do not be a hypocrite, but find evil in every man who is not Democratic. It is then you can see clearly the fog and mist that covers the land we live in.

Amen and Awomen.

CHAPTER FOUR

The Lost Resurrection
Of The Easter Bunny

One day the Easter Bunny was hop-hop-hopping down the bunny trail in the Garden of Gethsemane leaving eggs both white and multi-colored along the path. Now Mr. Gethsemane was not happy with the Easter Bunny littering his garden with such eggs. So Mr. Gethsemane called the local authorities who sent armed guards into the garden to arrest the Easter Bunny.

The Easter Bunny was not alone when they came to take him away. Some of the other woodland creatures were standing around the Easter Bunny with baskets full of eggs. As the armed guards approached the Easter Bunny they asked "Who has littered this garden with eggs?" A fox next to the Easter Bunny blurted out "The Easter Bunny! Him! Him! Him!" A rooster was not happy when one of the guards took hold of the Easter Bunny and threw an egg in the guard's face.

"Stop! Stop!" the Easter Bunny wiped the egg off the guard's face. All the other woodland creatures scattered leaving the Easter Bunny behind. The guards took the

Easter Bunny away for trial that very same day. He was found guilty for violation of environmental safety and spanked severely. Mr. Gethsemane protested on such a light sentence and demanded the death penalty because some of his animals choked on the eggs the Easter bunny left behind.

So the Easter Bunny was sentenced to death. What a mean thing for such a cute gray little bunny. There were few protests so the Easter Bunny was taken away and shoved into a rock hovel to die a lonely death. Two guards stood outside the rock hovel where a great stone was placed to keep the Easter Bunny confined.

Three days later the great stone fell over as the guards were fast asleep. The Easter Bunny did not hesitate for a second before leaving the darkness. However, boys and girls, the Easter Bunny would not be denied and when he came out of the darkness his fur was no longer gray, but white as snow. The Easter Bunny ran into the forest and into modern folklore history. He now comes out of his warren to entertain boys and girls all over the world for centuries to come on what is known now as Easter Bunny Sunday.

Would not the image of Christ be less threatening if His story was a simple fairy tale? A simple bunny story? If Jesus did not rise from the dead, what hope have we in an empty promise?

"If the dead will not come back to life again,
 then what point is there in people being baptized
 for those who are gone? Why do it unless you
 believe that the dead will some day rise again?"

I Corinthians 15: 28-30

If the Crucifixion and Resurrection are fairy stories in the line of the Easter Bunny and Santa Claus, what purpose do we serve in our belief? Will we water down the message because we displease the unbeliever? If they do not accept the truth let them stand before God and defend their position. Let us not condemn them out of our mouths if that condemnation makes no sense to them.

Shall we minimize the Resurrection? Shall we say it publicly that it may not have happened, but we hope so? Shall we cry out in these times:

"My God, My God why have you forsaken me?"

Mark 15: 34

Or do we stand up and say "Here I am, send me!" In the burial ceremony do we not say "Ashes to ashes, dust to dust...in the hope of the Resurrection to come."? It is not hope we seek, but verification of a promise by the Lord Jesus Christ Himself. Water down other promises if you want, but let us be relieved of our guilt and waiting for His call. I am still a sinner, but saved by You, my God and my Lord.

Do we deny the Resurrection so we do not offend the lost around us? We are here not only to offend, but to bring the lost to Christ. Not by force, but by truth and love expounded in God's Word. Jesus said "I am the Resurrection and the Life...." Okay, let's go. I believe in Your promise despite my shortcomings. I acknowledge Your right to the Crown. I only ask for, at the very least, a seat in a distant corner in Heaven rather than no seat at all. I can not profess to be worthy of your forgiveness, but a single tear from you is sufficient for my redemption. Believe only this and your life will be changed for the next rain of tears will be yours if you bow down before Christ. Cry out 'He has risen!' Yes He has, will you?

"I am amazed that you are turning away so soon from

God who, in His love and mercy, invited you to share the eternal life he gives through Christ; you are already

Following a different 'way to heaven', which really doesn't

go to heaven at all. For there is no other way than the one

we showed you; you are being fooled by those who twist

and change the truth concerning Christ."

Galatians 1: 6-9

The public outcry that the Cross is offensive, that the Christian faith is offensive to be heard, that the audacity of our forefathers to burden us with Christian moral obligations and that the Word of God has no place in society is unending. What do those who denigrate the faith offer that gives hope, freedom, salvation and peace? Again. I have read the Koran and it is not a book of peace, but one to convert by the sword to death or lifelong enslavement. Is that acceptable? Buddhism believes in no God at all. Reincarnation offers endless lives and endless despair.

What do we replace Christianity with that has guaranteed freedom of speech, press and religion? Christianity has had great tolerance of those who abuse those freedoms. It is the sin we abhor as does God although we tend to confuse condemning both the sin and sinner. The Bible is a blueprint for freedom, the Cross is the symbol of redemption not historical hypocrisy and the empty tomb the promise of eternal life. If there is anything else show me something better.

CHAPTER FIVE
Liberal Understanding
Of The Eternal Finiteness Of Life

In the vision of liberals view of religion and life God is a bigot and Jesus is just politically incorrect. It is believed to stop the insanity of berating homosexuals, fighting abortion, euthanasia and adultery we must pass laws that speak against the insanity. We all know that everyone has a free pass to heaven, however if you think about it hard enough this life or the next is meaningless, don't we?

For heaven's sake we hear that Jesus and His disciples were cross dressers and don't tell me they wore togas. God is a bigot because He has a long list of those who can not share His wealth, His wisdom or His forgiveness.

"Do you not know that the wicked will not inherit
the kingdom of God. Do not be deceived: Neither the
sexually immoral nor idolaters...."
I Corinthians 6: 9-10

The liberal says we need laws to curb this hate language so that the pulpit and conservative talk radio can be sanitized without being able to corrupt our youth. We must be tolerant and accepting for all those who live on this earth no matter what they've done against society. Who is God to tell us what to do? If we pass these laws it will show God who really is boss and show God how intolerant we can be towards Him and tear down the walls of heaven to get in if we must.

Is this the kind of ignorance and arrogance we can expect from those who lead our country? Do we allow the unfaithful to judge God and silence those who are faithful?

An example of this change is exemplified by the State of North Carolina who has considered that those giving testimony to use whatever book they hold sacred for their oath in court. Then they can tell the truth, the whole truth and nothing but the truth so help you in whatever spirit, truth or essential being you hold dear.

The books can be the Bible, Koran, Book of Mormon, and so on. In a society that holds religion to be separate from government how far down the chain do we go? Should we compromise by using a dictionary which has all the definitions of religion? Perhaps a Thesaurus to help with synonyms of each religion to ensure each one is as sacred as the other? Why not the Wall Street Journal for those who hold money sacred? Perhaps hold a dollar bill which would be the most convenient for any court system?

How do we accept testimony based on allegiance to faiths that have no respect for our government and its laws or those who believe in no god at all? How do we allow ourselves to change our standards of the law to accommodate each individual that refuses to accept American law and jurisprudence? We are becoming confused for the sake of political correctness to seek justice for all. Whether this statute has been accepted or not in North Carolina means nothing since it is the thought behind it.

Shall we be cowards in our faith when we allow the quiet death through capitulation in politics, religion and moral society? Shall we hide our faces when the roll call of Christians is heard throughout the land and the consequences of being called could mean imprisonment, ostracized from society or even death? Why Christ then? Why follow Him at all if we fear the Cross, fear the grave?

"For whoever wants to save his life
Shall lose it, but whoever loses his
Life for Me will save it."

Luke 9: 24

What manner of death is acceptable? Quietly in bed? Don't we all wish that? If our Lord had such an end we would not have to argue the point of separation of church and state. There would be no church and the state would only have one dictator after another. There would be no conscious to even think of good vs. evil for only evil would dictate the image of truth without justice, without love and without equality. There would be no arguments concerning abortion, euthanasia, gay rights or segregation. We would all equally be slaves. There would be no war for there would be nothing to fight over. There would be no constitution, no America, no refuge in prayer, no hope of eternal life, no future, no redemption only an open hole in the hearts of men and women.

What price liberty or the lack thereof? If we cannot stop the hand that chains us, what purpose is our freedom? What reason is faith if all we do is wait for divine intervention that will never come? We can not be subtle, we cannot be less than obnoxious in our belief in our faith, our country and the future for all free men. No longer can we turn the other cheek and expect our faith to be respected. We will suffer from our decision, but isn't that what Christ told us by picking up the Cross and following Him?

Excess taxation as proposed by our Congress inhibits, surely takes away life, liberty and the pursuit of happiness. Lenin would be proud taking down the mightiest nation on earth by three things: Taxes, taxes, taxes. We may have to render to Caesar what is Caesar's, but we do not have to allow Caesar to take away our livelihood. If the church speaks out against the excessiveness of Government will not Government shut it down?

We tend not to make that kind of sacrifice because of the luxury of being allowed to worship. I say luxury because if we had the duress that other countries are suffering from how many would still defiantly go to church?

The backbone of any nation is its faith, its moral stance and its compassion for the right future. Unfortunately, when it comes to God or mammon, mammon usually wins.

So now we come to basic humanism where God is a threat to freedom. For them believing in God is an embarrassment to most. They believe if God loves you, Jesus loves you then you are an ultra-right wing fanatic to be avoided and watched as a threat to their freedom of social disorder. To believe in God makes you bereft of reality and unable to make sane decisions. You, also, according to the humanist are unable to hold Public Office and certainly not the President of the United States or the U.S. Supreme Court. Of course that would mean no CEO's in business, a lawyer or any other higher position that could change the course of American history. To a humanist a Christian is like unto a demon, an enemy of freedom, patriotism, and the law.

We talk about freedom of speech but our freedom goes only so far. We can talk about anything, but not offend anyone. Why is there such a litany of hate at the mention of Jesus Christ unless He is such a threat to the haters way of life. Such guilt must cry out against God or it would have to acknowledge what they do is wrong.

Humanism believes more in science than faith. However, God is not only the Creator of Science it is science that explains God's Creation. In modern science God does not exist, only man has the clear knowledge of capacity to know of our existence and define the evidence of life. Science is the last line of defense of how man explains a finite god with no hope, no future, except as dust or mud of the earth to regenerate the circle of life.

Science is the truth test of being on our own. Scientific evidence refuses the existence of a Creator because of the skeletal findings that supposedly show evolution to be true. Thought the missing link between man and ape has not been found, it doesn't mean it doesn't exist. They believe it will be found and science will be vindicated while God vanishes into the fog of history.

No matter the uproar, the beating of chests, no matter the disbelief of the audacity of such a statement against all religions are false, the fact is God is God and no one or thing can replace Him. You cannot explain the workings of the universe without God because it is foolish and dangerous. If God is included, there can be no true comprehension. If God does not incorporate rules of natural law then moral and physical laws have no boundaries, no enforcement, nothing but arbitrary obedience which means nothing if God has no part in it. Ignoring God as Creator is lying to yourself because you will always be looking over your shoulder wondering if it really was just talk. Men and women need direction. However, the finite direction to the grave is not one to be glorified in a race without a finish line for the winner.

Atheists say they do not believe in God. They fight to disprove the existence of God, try to fight for legislation against prayer, the bible in schools and any mention of God in government or public gatherings. If God doesn't exist why do they try so hard to prove it? Why take God from others if you truly believe He doesn't exist? So why not just laugh at us so we can return the favor later on when they stand before Him?

The problem with non-Christians, anti-God militants is that they attack the Creator and the sinner. A sinner's past is suspect and easier to attack than God and the Scriptures. When the faith cannot be dissected, the man must be put on the table.

You cannot, you will not expunge the Word of God. Russia tried it and failed. China has tried it and the faith still grows. Most of the countries that were behind the iron curtain failed to silence the Word of God. Hatred for Jesus Christ is irrational, ignorant of His coming and illogical passion for spiritual suicide. Jesus represents freedom to think, eternal life, redemption, peace, eternal love and satisfaction in the life one leads. No other religion has that for no other faith away from God does the same.

We are basically selfish in a me-me-me world. Life is too short, we are not rich enough, we are not happy in our relationships, our job, our free time, nothing satisfies us I that need to be loved and honored. Everything stinks in a world we live in because we are not the focus. With God and our Lord Jesus the focus is two things, Him and us.

Those who do not believe strive for success only to find a wormhole into oblivion. They talk of souls, but leave out the fact that we each have one that needs to be saved, not wasted. If given the choice of possible happiness in this life or the expected happiness in the next life they will pick the former over the latter almost every time. Their view of happiness is if it feels good, do it. If it gives you a warm fuzzy feeling, watch it. If it relieves your grief and pain, swallow it. If it keeps you from feeling alone, embrace it.

Our world confines God to second class citizenship. We put God in our pocket instead of pinning him to our lapels. When things are well we reach into our pockets, set God in the palm of our hands and say God has truly blessed us. When things go wrong we reach into our pockets and find only lint and change. We do not know how to defend our faith in bad times neither can the church teach you more than putting a smile on your face through diversity. Is this the power of humanism or atheism you want for your future? When you see no light at the end of a tunnel, will you rejoice in the darkness or call out for a helping Hand?

CHAPTER SIX
Churches- keep the faith....to yourself

Life as a Christian is a survival till the last breath in a journey not of disguise and silent infiltration, but of wearing armor, prayer and raising the sword, the Bible, of Christ. The fight sometimes is subtle and sometimes obvious. Those who do not believe wish to silence the voice of God. You are that voice and if you do not answer against the cry to defy God, you accept the denial of Christ. You stand on the edge of the pit of Stephen and allow the stoning to continue. We are in the age of Spiritual mazes, a world that hates Christ and wishes to obliterate the strength of Scripture by using reinterpretation to suit the moral abyss of the world.

Let us not confuse the issue of the church by bringing Jesus Christ into the argument. For the words of Christ redefine the cloudy interpretation that we all know and love today into a crystal clear vision of God's purpose in our lives. Why should we not stay confused and enjoy our disillusionment that keeps us wandering in the dark? It gives us the faint hope that God will let us sneak under the gates of Heaven because of our self ignorance.

We are asked to be tolerant of those things that God does not tolerate. We are entering the early stages of the last days where Christianity is an abomination to many and even worse neutralized within its pulpits. Are we shadows looking for the light that filters through images of the church windows? Light is a healing hand to the darkness that envelopes us. Many in the pews feel that darkness more because of the fractured direction of the church. The pulpit has become confusing anagrams and legends of the lost with its doctrine on a pedestal with wheels constantly moving from right to left depending on the political winds of change. How can anyone stop and make a stand if the church drifts further away from the Word of God? Scripture is easy to misinterpret, but it is hard to stand still and say this is what God said and I will stand with Him.

Why are we cowards for Christ instead of the soldiers of Christ? I do not mean soldiers so we kill the infidels who do not believe as it preaches in the Koran. Missionaries all over the world stay in dangerous places to preach the gospel and the only weapon they have is the Bible. Much of the world sees that weapon, called Scripture, as more dangerous than a nuclear bomb or socialism in a democratic nation.

One thing they are right about and that is Christianity is the most powerful and dangerous religion in the world. Why?

"For God so loved the world that He gave His only Begotten Son, that whosoever believeth in Him shall not perish, but have everlasting life." John 3:16

Christ can change every last human being into a holy temple and God can crush this world with His fist. No bomb, no weapon of mass destruction can ever match His power. Revelation tells us that we win in the end yet we worry about a third world war. So we doubt and that doubt is used by our enemies to demoralize us and control our actions. We deserve to suffer if we doubt. We deserve to have indecision if we doubt. We deserve to lose our freedoms if we doubt.

What is the circular motion of life? Is it dust to dust and whatever happens in between is an accident and circumstances that are soon to be forgotten? We want to be remembered. We yearn to be remembered for something, anything. Why else are we here? Sheer happenstance is what many want us to believe. Who would not want to join Lincoln, Roosevelt, or Washington?

History swallows whole lifetimes without a second thought. We are only a sigh, a blink of an eye or a passing thought. Great nations have all churned themselves into the dustbin of history. Many more will join the dust. Our nation and the world are at a crossroads where common sense is rare. Our Republic feels the horses of change pulling it away into a more socialistic society which has never succeeded in the past. The key to resisting the urge to take the wrong road is through knowing past history where socialism led to totalitarianism. In order for a socialist system to work it would have to shut down and nullify the church. There would have to be someone in charge and that someone wields the power over millions without freedom of speech, press or religion.

To lock out the destruction from within, the church it must be the moral backbone of any society only if it is not morally corrupt itself. The church cannot be politically correct if it is to succeed in curtailing the moral abyss our country is running towards. The church can easily become the slinky of our moral fabric if it bends in the wind of political correctness.

Good Christian men turn into penny vampires to justify their thirst for greed and power believing that their wealth is given through God's blessing. That is both a true and untrue statement. God wants you to be the best in your field but not for the sole purpose of making yourself wealthy and lord yourself over less fortunate Christians.

"For it is difficult for a wealthy man to enter the kingdom of heaven as a camel through the eye of a needle."
Luke 18:25

There are many issues that the church must speak out against, yet those in power will not accept it. They allow us to speak out, but not about abortion, euthanasia, stem cell research, gay marriages, and certainly if we must speak, not in public. We, as Christians, have set up our own groups within our fellowships. First is the W.I.M.P.S. or Wandering Individuals Mumbling Platitudes Silently. The second group is the C.Y.S.T.S. or Check Your Spirit Treasure Seasonally. Third is the F.I.N.K.S. or False Identification Never Knows the Spirit. Fourth is the P.I.N.K.I.E. or Put In Nothing, Know It Exceptionally. Fifth is the G.O.U.R.D.S. or Gossipers Of Unusual Resourcefulness Denying Salvation. There are a number of categories to choose from and each one can be an organization unto itself.

There is a cultural battle within our country and those who struggle with the question of right vs. wrong are finding that there seems to be no wrong answer. There appears to be no absolutes, only gray areas where shadows of hypocrisy live and breathe. The Christian church has been identified as the plague of this nation by those who fear its absolutes. However, Christians can no longer explain and defend the basic absolutes of our faith.

One absolute is that Jesus is the Christ, the Son of the Living God. A second absolute is that Christ rose from the dead on the third day after which hundreds saw him and talked with Him. The third absolute is in the Scripture verse John 14:6, "I am the Way the Truth and the Life; no man comes to the Father but through Me."

A major difference between Christians and non-Christians is the way we think in a given situation. An example would be in a question put to me when I was in college: "If Christ went to the cross willingly, did He not commit suicide?" The discussion afterwards was not that it was ridiculous, but some thought it a valid question. When we ponder such things as the DaVinci Code where we think such a message is possible, we have lost our direction.

Do we have to be so concerned about the DaVinci Code controversy? Yes, for it has shown the biblical ignorance of both Christians and non-Christians alike.

"For false Christs and false prophets will appear and perform great signs and miracles to deceive even the elect-if that were possible."

Matthew 24: 24

It seems it would take a lot less to deceive the elect and it is possible. If we do not read God's Word we can and will be deceived even if one or two words were changed so the scripture sounds right, but its meaning is completely changed.

If someone says to you "It is a matter of interpretation." He or she is really saying "I do not accept the truth because I would have to make a decision in my life. I do not want to make that decision now or at any other time and this statement keeps me in my own comfort zone." Is it a matter of interpretation that a famous actor, statesman, author or relative go to heaven because they are famous or a loved one? Is it a matter of interpretation that a practicing homosexual lead the church because we must be tolerant and loving to all? God is intolerant to all things He says is wrong.

"Do you not know that the wicked
will not inherit the Kingdom of God? Do not
be deceived:
　　　Neither the sexually immoral nor
idolaters nor male prostitutes nor
homosexual offenders
　　　nor thieves nor the greedy nor
swindlers will
　　　inherit the Kingdom of God. And that
is what some
　　　of you were. But you were washed,
you were sanctified
　　　in the name of the Lord Jesus Christ
and by the Spirit of God."
I Corinthians 6: 9-11

　　　Yes! God does not tolerate those who
do these things and do not believe in Him,
rebel against His Word and sin against His
Spirit. That these sins can be washed away
is the reality of Christ. If you reject Him out
of hand, as it is your right, then why would
you be surprised on Judgment Day for His
condemnation? How many souls plead when
it is too late for mercy? Then cry when our
Lord tells them as in Rev. 3: 15-17:

　　　"I know your deeds, that you are
neither cold
　　　nor hot, I wish you were either one or
the other!

So, because you are lukewarm-neither hot nor cold-

I am about to spit you out of my mouth. You say, 'I

Am rich, I have acquired wealth and do not need a

thing.' But you do not realize that you are wretched.

Pitiful, poor, blind and naked."

Many in the church have accepted the lie of tolerance concerning homosexuality, abortion and doctor assisted suicide. Some in the church supported the starving of Teri Schiavo which was Euthanasia a so called mercy killing. Many stand for abortion thought the bible preaches against the killing of innocents. Will you be the one of the ones who stand before the Lord and say in your defense I am one with you Lord:

"Not everyone who says to me, "Lord,

Lord" will enter the Kingdom of Heaven,

but only he who does the will of My Father who is in Heaven. Many will say to me on that day, "Lord, Lord, did we

not prophesy in your name, and in your name drive out demons and perform many demons and perform may miracles?" Then

I will tell them plainly, 'I never knew you. Away from me, you evildoers.'"

Matthew 7: 21-23

By all means, let us not confuse the issue of the church by bringing Jesus Christ into the argument. For the words of Christ define the cloudy interpretation that we all know and love today into a crystal clear vision of God's purpose in our lives. Why should we not stay confused to enjoy our disillusionment and misunderstanding that keeps us wandering in the dark? It gives us the faint hope that God will let us sneak under the gate of Heaven because of our ignorance.

The last thing a Christian wants is to not be seen in the blur of life. To that end, we are not here for the worship of the church, but of God. We are a Christian nation no matter what the A.C.L.U. says, no matter what the mass media writes and no matter what public education teaches. Darwin was wrong. George Washington and Abraham Lincoln were right. A lie is not the truth if it is a lie and the facts support the truth.

Where do we start our fight against ignorance? What is the Word of God? Is it a myth, fiction or truth? If it is a myth than there is no hope or

future. If it is fiction than it is the most convincing deception man has ever conceived. If it is truth than we are refusing to follow it. Myth is hard to justify since there are too many historical facts involved with the telling. Fiction is easier to accept, but why has there not been evidence to challenge it? How do we accept an all-powerful supernatural being when that power is seemingly so quiet, so far away?

We accept, by faith, the steadying hand of God that holds back the evil in this world. The evil comes from free choice, free will because it is the nature of man to challenge any authority. It is because of this challenge that the pulpit has changed in many ways as a sounding board for various Theological arguments.

We must be clear that we are not carnival barkers hawking for Christ with shouts of He is here or He is there. Yet we hear many beckoning with winning smiles to 'Come to me and I will help you reap the harvest. Are you heavy laden? Then diet on the scraps of my blessed table of wisdom. Are you suffering in the Spirit? Then take this magical elixir of angelic antacid. Does death frighten you? Then don't look in the mirror for it is only a glass darkly.'

The true How-to book is the Bible and the worst a church can offer its members and visitors are moderate indifference to its teachings. When our Lord is attacked in the media do we just shake our heads and cluck our tongues? Moderate indifference. When the church allows Political Correctness to water down the message of the scriptures we are accepting moderate indifference to the Spirit. I say moderate indifference because we care, but not enough to do anything about it most of the time.

We give the impression that our Lord is not worthy for us to kneel down and fold our hands in submission. We pray with our hands in our pockets, eyes open and minds mouthing words of truth in monotones. Where is the fervor for the Lord, the faith of our fathers and the yearning of the Spirit to see God's face? Are we too content, too successful or abject failures looking for pity?

"Then he said to them, 'Watch out! Be on your guard against all kinds of greed; a man's life does not consist in the abundance of his possessions.'"

Luke 12: 15

Go to Africa, China and the Middle East to ask those dying for their faith if we are truly blest to worship when and where we please. How many of us if asked the question "Are you a Christian?" with a gun pointed at our heads and would say "Yes."

Why should we believe our faith is proved by our checkbooks, our tribulation is being asked to work in the nursery, our passport to heaven is attendance in church on Sunday and martyrdom is adding Sunday evening services and singing in the choir.

Where are the scars of the whip from our taskmasters? Where is the Cross that burdens our backs as we walk to Golgotha? Do we walk with Christ to Emmaus? It is certainly easier to back away from controversy than to sit in its center. It is safer to blend in with those around us, but we are the salt of the earth. Yet we do not want confrontation because we cannot defend the faith intelligently. Many of us are Biblically ignorant and if ignorance is bliss we are very happy Christians.

Why risk our jobs to witness even if the opportunity arises? Why lose friends because we offend them with our faith? Why risk our lives to be missionaries in countries who clearly do not want us? Why lay our lives down if we do not trust God to hold us up in our faith? If Christ is not truly with us, then it is better to hide from those who may persecute us.

If we are unworthy to have Christ to forgive us, then we do not understand His coming. Yes, we are unworthy when we come to accept Him, but our unworthiness flows throughout scripture which soon gives us the strength to forgive ourselves as well. We need to stand upright to adversity if issues are Biblically wrong. We must so say. We are not politically correct because Christianity will not survive if our spirit bends in the wind with social change.

Jesus the Christ was crucified because He did not make concessions. Why is it that so many curse our Lord because He will not concede anything that is not of God? The unbeliever says we must have compassion for all people. I agree, but not if the compassion compromises the Word of God. Sounds fanatical? Yes, it does! Anytime you stand for the truth without compromise is considered fanatical. Real fanatics are those that insist that the Bible needs to be adjusted to save everyone no matter their sin, no matter what they believe and no matter what ethereal being they follow. What faith is worth believing if there is no line in the sand that you do not cross?

Who will believe in a God that is ruled by political or religious polls? Who will follow a God that is indecisive? Gog is God because He tells us these are the rules, obey them and you will receive eternal life. What are the rules?

"I am the Way, the Truth, and the Life;
No man comes to the Father, but through Me."

John 3:16

Christian anarchy is not the answer to our society's ills. Christian unity through responsibility, faith, courage and leadership will prove that the Lord our God will bring stability and prosperity to our nation. If our churches split over moral or political issues, how are we witnessing to others? We are no different than corporations or businesses who exist for profit and shareholding. We squabble like those in congress who bed this way and that depending on the lobbyists influence.

A personal note must be inserted here. In 1977, at the age of 27, I was asked to be an elder in my church. The pastor, at my very first meeting, brought up a discussion and vote concerning whether practicing homosexuals should be allowed to teach Sunday School or hold office. I immediately started the firestorm with the fact that the Bible prohibits this kind of thing. Why should there be any discussion at all? The elder to my right said "Not everyone believes in the Bible." Then my pastor said "It is a matter of what the congregation thinks how we deal with this issue." I said, and I think I hold the record for being an elder for only twenty minutes, "If the Bible is not a reason for our decision, then I will vote against allowing practicing homosexuals in leadership of this church and I respectfully resign." I then walked out.

Carnal Christians have no effect on society except to decimate the calling of Christ. Politically correct Christians destroy our government and society. Why would someone want to be a Christian if they are going be just as miserable as you are? If Christians are miserable, they express that misery in their jobs, their homes and their church. Who needs that?

Education is key for all ages. We cannot ignore our history, our faith, our constitution and expect to survive. Socialism will never work since it is the enemy of Christianity. Liberal acceptance of all things contrary to scripture will only bring anarchy and financial disaster. We cannot make our country turn into puzzle pieces of ethnic diversity without a common language or common cultural history. This is not to ignore the ethnic history of those who have come here, but that history does not supersede our own. We want freedom as long as it is not from our founding fathers and not focused on our religious heritage. Our states cannot turn into separate nations defying the country as a whole. We cannot rebel against our heritage and beliefs without losing our strength and identity. So, too, our churches are splitting into fractious pieces that have interlocking sides that present a kaleidoscope of interpretations. No wonder non-Christians feel need to be saved. If you are a mirror image of those you want to save, what changes are necessary for them to follow Christ?

CHAPTER SEVEN

What? More about Churches....How droll!

What life is there if there is no life at all? If our lives do not lead to another life we live in continuous darkness. How many of us are flat liners on God's EKG machine? It is not easy to believe, to have faith in a Being that is everywhere in time and space. That Being seems to be nowhere that we can see or touch. We feel Him in prayer and we know Him through Jesus Christ. The truth is that Jesus the Christ walked the earth, spoke in God's voice and became a black hole for our sins. Whenever He comes into our lives the black hole he created sucks our sins into another dimension never to return.

We, as part of the greatness of the church, as Christians, need to remember God's words from Isaiah 55 that "My ways are not your ways." You want to be politically correct in accepting gay clergy, gay marriages, euthanasia and abortion, but God does not have to be politically correct.

What is the result that we are looking for in our faithfulness in Christ? Is it wealth? Healing? One step up in the hierarchy of the church we attend? More friends? Less stress? A sudden overwhelming urge to go to the mission field? We tend to get none of these things if we look to use faith for own gratification. Nothing we have is our own, but God's. If we use what God has given us in secret is that what is meant by laying treasures in heaven?

"Lay not up for yourselves treasures upon earth,
where moth and rust doth corrupt, and where thieves
break through and steal; but lay up for yourselves treasures in heaven, where
neither moth nor rust corrupt, and where thieves do not break through nor
steal."

Matthew 6: 19,20

How easy it is to mock those who believe in heaven and hell which we know to be true. How easy it is to mock those ethereal places of goodness and light, golden streets and comfortable mansions or the pit of fire, rooms of redundancy or the blackness of eternal night separated from God. We can not comprehend in an enlightened society that the children's fairy book called the Holy Bible has any significance to our own adult life. We do not cower from the threat of damnation rather we are indifferent. We do not stand for the glorification of God, we merely make a show for a few hours a week. The awe of God is just a passing cloud that rains on us now and again with either mercy or casual judgment.

Only fools believe that God is seen to be a phantom that lies in dark corners only to appear when we do something wrong. God is not a "gotcha" Being waiting for us to sin and point out our shortcomings. God is not an "I told you so" Being or a fire and brimstone mercenary except when things get out of hand such as Sodom and Gomorrah.

God is more of a "What were thinking?" Lord. God is judge and jury through scripture. When we stand before God after our lives are through we will hear the scripture that we condemn ourselves in the offences and defiance of what we knew was right, but decided not to obey. We will be condemned by our own words and actions. Who will testify on our behalf? If there is silence it is because the only One who could testify on our behalf, Jesus Christ, we have rejected in this life. Jesus will not know you and all the pleading in eternity will not change that then.

"I know your works; you are neither cold

Nor hot. Would that you were cold or hot!

So, because you are lukewarm, and
neither cold nor hot, I will spew you out of
my mouth."

Revelation 3: 15,16

"Not everyone who says to me, 'Lord,
Lord,'
shall enter the Kingdom of Heaven,
but he who does the will of my Father who
is in heaven.
On that day many will say to me, 'Lord,
Lord did we not prophesy in your
name, and cast out
demons in your name, and do many
mighty works
in your name? And then will I declare
to them,
'I never knew you; depart from me,
you evildoers.'"

Matthew 7: 21-23

How much clearer can the Lord be
than to tell you that "We never talked. We
never once walked the same path. You never
looked for Me, but used My name for your
gain. How could you have known Me, if I
did not know you?" Is this the conversation
you want to have with our Lord?

We find common sense is found easier
in the dictionary than practiced in real life.
Common sense means rational behavior and

personal responsibility. Unfortunately, it appears to be invoked only in times of madness and war. When it is sought the images of right and wrong become blurred while the conversation veers toward debate within the shadow of hypocrisy lingering in a dark corner.

We hear crying within the rooms beyond us, but as we enter the crying stops for a moment before beginning again in the next room. We wonder who can be so sorrowful and why we can not help them. As the years go by the crying is louder, but now more familiar. We are tired of searching the reason for the tears and ignore the unhappiness. We begin to weaken with age and despair of what could have been as we start to cry. It is then we hear the footsteps outside our door where we panic and escape to the next room. Finally, we understand, almost too late, the crying we heard in our youth was the tears from our old age. The next generation is trying to comfort us, but we are too ashamed to accept the truth.

What is it you want to say to God as a Christian? That our Lord Jesus the Christ suffered and died for us, rose again so we might rise again with

Him and it is not enough? Do we expect to be all King's Kids whereby we exert our spiritual prowess based on wealth, power and prestige? And if we do not have any of these fine attributes have we failed in our Christian walk? Many Christians are poor, many Christians do not have a voice in their church or community and many Christians are not looked up to because they live day to day relying on God to help them through unscathed.

Unscathed in sin, wrapped in small blessings and hoping for a kind word from out of the void of society. Many walk with scars unseen because they choose not to complain for complaining only hardens the hearts around them

The modern church looks upon a poor man as spiritually lacking in faith and blessings. The church expects pillars of society, but we forget that the disciples were sentenced to death, in poverty and in prison by those in power. We can not base spiritual success in terms of money, property or political power.

First, we must speak of the political sense in order for the church to survive the 21st century. It must not change with the society in which it lives. Yet, it has with accepting women as ministers and priests which cause a small tremor, but not a major problem. Now homosexuals are given the "privilege" of being pastors, priests and even bishops bringing the church another step toward spiritual ennui. The church does not condemn sin, but ignores or rationalizes it so that the coffers do not go empty. Is this the true future of the church? Will changes like this help society embrace Christianity?

The act of homosexuality is the most selfish act one can perform on another. It gratifies only in mutual masturbation where there can be no conception only narcissistic orgasm.

Did we not hear Bishop Robinson who said it best on ABC News that "Homosexuality is a special gift from God." Acceptance and tolerance of homosexuality within the church is necessary for the future and true respectability of all religions, is it not? I choose not.

"Do you not know that the wicked will not
inherit the kingdom of God? Do not be deceived; Neither the sexually immoral,
nor idolaters nor adulterers nor male prostitutes
nor homosexual offenders nor thieves nor the greedy nor drunkards nor slanderers
nor swindlers will inherit the kingdom of God."

I Corinthians 6: 9

The goal of every church is to be successful balancing budgets and filling the pews however possible hopefully with those whose jobs can give ten percent or more. In accepting all walks of life and lifestyles shows a growing maturity that will honor God in His ever-changing openness to His people. The only good Christian is a rich Christian syndrome has pervaded our churches. The Lord offers richness in the Spirit more than richness in wealth.

This does not mean that Christians can not be wealthy, but it is their spirit on how they handle their wealth that is the key to their faith. It is not a proof that if you are blessed with wealth that you are blessed in Spirit. God's love is not assured in tax brackets unless He is a Democrat. What then is expected of us as Christians?

"Take nothing for the journey-no staff, no bag, no bread, no money, no extra tunic. Whatever house you enter, stay there until you leave that town. If people do not welcome you, shake the dust off your feet when you leave their town. If people do not welcome you, shake the dust off your feet when you leave their town as a testimony against them."

Luke 9: 3-5

Good Christian men turn into penny vampires to justify their thirst for greed and power believing that their wealth is given through God's blessing. That is both true and an untrue statement. God wants you to be the best in your field, but not to the sole purpose of making you wealthy.

Rely on the Lord your God because it does not mean financial success will authenticate your faith. It does not mean that successful Christians are bad Christians, but there is a tendency to look down on those less fortunate, less educated. A greater temptation is that you believe you have secured your ticket to heaven. Once saved always saved is relegated to God to judge not man. Being a King's Kid is a myth if wealth is your measure of a man or woman. Does being a King's Kid mean acting like a spoiled brat? Is there a divine deletion of Christians who walk the path of Christ, but do not see His footprints? Do we hold sacred only those scriptures that uplift rather than condemn our actions? Are you divine slaves that allow everyone to walk all over you turning you cheek over and over again? Do we try to make Christian soldiers, but with only a feminine touch? Do we open condensed Bibles and surrender before the battle has started? Many third world nations have Christians living in poverty and being persecuted to death for their belief in Christ. How much richer are they?

Churches are a place of worship and not a place for politics you say? Who says? Issues of national importance such as abortion, pornography, euthanasia, taxes and homosexuality are moral and spiritual issues. The church is told it is not an institution to cause grief for the government or society. The church is told that it must accept those things which scripture does not and must co-exist with the rest of society. The courts decide moral and ethical behavior that corrupt the church. Separation of Church and State abuses the church so that it can not have the desired impact that God wishes it to have. What is the answer to the lethargy of our faith?

"You are the salt of the earth, but if the salt

loses its saltiness, how can it be made salty

again? It is no longer good for anything,

except to be thrown out and trampled by men."

Matthew 5: 13

Is the church then a place of scripture reading, except for those parts that incite vicious debate over those same themes mentioned above. Should the church not have its hands in the courtroom, schools, government, media or theater. The Supreme Court has stated that there is to be a separation of Church and State so that even the mere mention of Jesus Christ constitutes grounds for dismissal of teachers in school and sending up a red flag for those seeking office. How do we answer this absurdity?

"You are the light of the world. A city on a hill can not be hidden.
Neither do people light a lamp and put it under a bowl. Instead they put it on its
stand and it gives light to everyone in the house. In the same way let your light
shine before men, that they may see your good deeds and praise your Father in
heaven."
Matthew 5: 14-16

School prayer was banned in schools to keep faith outside the classroom. Thursday used to be times of religious instruction in the 60's, but now mostly banned for moral instruction as seen fit by the local school boards and government. Moral instruction now includes condoms, sexual variations, and birth control. Ethical and moral behavior outlined in God's Word precludes the necessity of such instruction, God is a subversive and a killjoy in the glory of sexual intimacy so can not be the author of such instruction is what has been determined by the courts.

The addition of gay ministers and lesbian pastors supposedly show a progressive behavior in the pulpit. It tries to show tolerance and fairness to all walks of life despite the narrowness and bigotry of scripture. How does God answer this?

"For such are false apostles, deceitful workers, transforming themselves into the
    apostles of Christ. And no marvel. For Satan himself is transformed into an angel of
    light. Therefore it is no great thing if his ministers also be transformed as the
    ministers of righteousness; whose end will be according to his works."
II Corinthians 11: 13-15

Atheists say they do not believe in God. They fight to disprove the existence of God even though their belief suggests strongly that there is nothing to disprove in the first place. They fight for legislation against prayer, the Bible in schools and any mention of God in Government or public places. If God doesn't exist why do they try so hard to prove it? Why not just ignore His existence and God will do the same? Why take God from others if you believe He doesn't exist?

The moral backbone of our country has osteoporosis. We do not have the calcium of Scripture, American History, Literature or Government Studies. We instead have deleted history of the pilgrims and the American Revolution because many quotes refer to God, religious history, taxes and individual freedom. Classical literature reinforces the faith of our fathers and recent literature dictates the insane declaration of Separation of Church and State. How can we separate our decisions in any walk of life if we are truly free?

Life everlasting now involves cryogenics, a good life equals a free pass to heaven and any famous person can enter heaven no matter his faith or religion. We need lists to know what is right and wrong. Would a list help us understand right from wrong?

Right	**Wrong**
Heterosexual marriage	Gay marriage
Literal Translation	Judicial Translation
Patriotic allegiance	Separation of church & state

Low taxes to encourage saving & buying
                    High taxes to stifle Capitalism

Capitalism   Socialism

Three R's in school
                    Political correctness in education

American history   Revised history

Law & Order   Chaos & Anarchy

Equality for all
                    Equality for all except Christians

Encouragement for a positive role
                                        Discouragement

Abstinence   Handing out condoms
                                        & birth control

Respect for things   Lack of respect

Freedom of speech regarding Jesus Christ/God
                    Freedom of speech with the
                    caveat that it cannot include
                    God except as a curse, or a
                    generic view of a universal
                                        being

There that does it, I feel better already.

CHAPTER EIGHT
Win-win situation

As Christians we sometimes hope those who abuse us will go to Hell. However, if they become Christians their guilt of abusing us may never go away.

Showing right from wrong is an ambiguity. Recent literature and tolerance can only be centered in everything but the Bible which is an antiquated morality play signifying nothing in its view. Christianity is not subject for discussion except by those less enlightened. God is a myth in this kind of literature, a frightening image like a bully in a school or the bogeyman hiding in closets watching your every move. Do you think this is true?

We all must be like Martin Luther in saying 'Here I stand I can do no other.' And mean it! If we do not our churches will fail, be corrupted and useless to the lost. If you do not stand and read the bible and then you have lost your armor, your sword and your shield. If you do not speak against ungodly things, you condone them as Paul watched Stephen being stoned. If you fear those who speak against the Lord, then you stand naked in your faith.

We are in an age of candles looking for a flame. The Lord is that flame which we can extinguish within ourselves or let it burn brightly so the darkness will have to yield to the light. How can the light conquer despair if the candle will not put forth the flame? The darkness is not unconquerable even if you are the only one with the light.

How can you stand if you are crippled with guilt? How can you speak of Christ if your tongue is numb? How can you hear if you are deaf to the whispers of God? When fear has control of your thoughts it spreads to your mouth, your eyes and your ears. Your mouth will not speak of Christ, your eyes will not see the miracles of faith and your ears will not hear the Word of God. You become not a soldier for Christ, but a zombie.

We have the 'Peter Pan' syndrome in Christian churches. We want to be children of God instead of men and women in Christ. To grow up brings more responsibility and accountability. To stay as children of God we can use excuses and apologies to live our lives. To say 'Yes, I have sinned, please forgive me." is embarrassing, but necessary

As children of God we use the excuse 'I am new in the faith.' The answer comes back 'but you have been a child of God for thirty years! When will you grow up to be an adult in Christ?' Then we cry and have tantrums that pointing out their sins is not

Christ-like and how ashamed we should be for pointing out their weaknesses when we have so many blah, blah, blah, blah. Then the child of God flies to Neverland instead of scripture and prayer where it is safe and comfortable in their ignorance.

Why do you go to church? Do you feel a dull thud in your chest that you want to change? Are you that candle looking for a flame? Have you used the cigarette lighter of money, power and prestige only to be frustrated because that light usually flickers in the wind and is extinguished? The light of Jesus Christ burns through the strongest of winds and the tempests of despair in our lives.

There is no way to understand the logic of faith or the mystery of God. We believe that there a force that drives us or there are angels watching over us. One is more comforting than the other. When one mentions the Holy Bible or Jesus Christ do you get a thrill inside you or that same dull thud?

We cannot justify heaven for those who do not believe in Jesus Christ no matter how much we love them. Simple truth is that we try to reinterpret scripture based on feelings for someone else. My father had bone cancer and dying in the late 90's. He was excommunicated from the Catholic

Church because he would not bring us kids up in the Catholic faith. He blamed God and the church for his failures in life and marriage. Even on the day of his death my father did not accept Christ as his savior. I wrote a letter telling him that I learned much from him and that God loved him despite what he thought. What effect it had on him, I do not know. I sadly cannot say if I will see him in heaven. It may be a harsh statement, but I know neither my mother nor older brother who were killed by my younger brother died without salvation. God has given us ample time to decide. It is our choice until it is time we stand before God who makes the final decision for us. That decision will neither be lukewarm or politically correct.

In the past you could solve arguments by discussion, but you cannot argue with someone who says 'I don't care' or 'That's your point of view and mine is just as valid.' One problem with this is that there are inherent truths, there is right or wrong no matter whether you care or not. If someone pulls a gun on you, you don't say "I don't care." If someone hates you and threatens you, you don't say "Well, that's your point of view."

We are a society of self-fulfillment where God has no part. Our churches are dying, barbarians are filling the seats as the choirs sing while the congregation disintegrates into a sitcom of Punch and Judy. Is this what you see in your church? Do you believe we cannot rely on God alone because He is just out of reach and faith is not good enough? Do you have to "feel" God's presence? Do you "enjoy" God's spirit? Must we enter the gates of Heaven not only with thanksgiving, but hugs, kisses, gold stars on our heads and grateful Jesus who is thankful you bothered to show up? Are you the center of the universe?

Do we have to feel prickly with goose bumps of song and the tears from a sad message? Do we need a message of death, despair and desperation that ultimately triumphs in the glorification of the Jesus experience lifting our arms upward and speaking in gibberish tongues that even the angels cannot understand.

Since when are real Christians a danger to society? Since when have Christians been suspect when running for political positions? Since when are real Christians a danger to the judiciary? Why can't Christians run industry? Since when should Christians hide in the same closets where homosexuals have escaped from? What walls should we build to hide our light from the rest of society? We are to be the salt of the earth not the artificial sweetener to stir into the immorality and chaos of this world. The path to Christ does not lead into a maze, but a narrow road that is straight and right to a definite end.

Do we pray hoping not to hear an answer for how awesome and fearsome is prayer if God answers us? Prayer is not a series of numbers or gibberish that many call prayer language. God is not an author of confusion so why do we confuse those around us who do not have the gift of interpreting gibberish? Even Christians with the gift of interpretation would be hard pressed to understand what was being said. The object of prayer language is to draw attention to the speaker and easier for that speaker to join in without commitment to a specific need or issue. It is perfectly Politically Correct

Do not blurt out something to impress those around you with your hidden spirituality for the silence afterwards sends the message of confusion and doubt. If you are insulted by these comments, good. We need to speak clearly of God's love, our faith, His blessing and sacrifice for the world to understand that our God is an awesome God.

CHAPTER NINE
Global Warming
Pffft!

Global warming is now blamed on CO_2 and the need to lower gaseous effects that is destroying our planet. We are in dire need of a solution to slow down the process. It amazes me that CO_2 is the enemy since it is the prime nourishment to keep plants alive and wonder of wonders to keep us alive, too! Where does oxygen come from but the very trees and plants we wish to starve? I have a better suggestion that would slow the process down.

1) Everyone in the world hold their breath for two minutes four times a day
2) Take Beano before every meal.
3) Eat no gaseous foods like baked beans, green pepper, or broccoli. No carbonated drinks.
4) Plant more trees.
5) Ride bicycles
6) Demand politicians have a code of silence.

There, I've solved the problems of global warming and if I am wrong:

"There will be signs in the sun, moon, and stars.

On the earth, nations will be in anguish and

perplexity at the roaring and tossing of the sea.

Men will faint from terror, apprehensive of what is coming on the

world, for the heavenly bodieswill be shaken. At that time they will see the Son

of Man coming in a cloud with power and great glory. When these things begin to

take place, stand up and lift up your heads, because your redemption

is drawing near."

Luke 21: 25-28

CHAPTER TEN

Save the children, save the Spotted Owl
Save the chickens and pigs, but
kill the fetuses

Fetus! There's a fetus in the room! We're all going to die! That's right I'm not having a baby, I'm having a fetus and it is terminal! It's not a baby bump, but a piece of disruptive tissue in a biological tsunami!

When is a child not a child? When it is helpless in the mother's womb. Abortion's other name is Political Fetus Genocide from a nation with conflicting images of narcissism and self-hatred where we hug ourselves so hard in ego gratification that we cut off the blood of reason. We have no room for others to take our place. Mini-me's are a threat to our pleasure, our income and our time. We are selfish and conceded that life is the focal point of existence both our own and everyone else's that surround us.

Abortion is the most controversial subject in the nation. It is controversial because it is out of guilt that those who support it are unable to justify the killing of innocent children. Abortion is based on the general thought that what is in a woman's womb is subject to the will of that woman and no one else. It is her choice to abort the fetus or mass of tissue which supposedly has no feelings, no sense of life, but just a piece of gunk or a congealed tar pit until the first gasp of air or the first cry in a doctor's hand.

Where do we get this sense that if it's not seen or heard, it doesn't exist if we do not want it to exist? How do we make any woman believe that the gunk in her body is bad and it is inconvenient to ruin her life so it must be expelled from her body? Are women taught that an unnecessary pregnancy is worse than having cancer? Is the issue of abortion about a woman's health, her lifestyle, and/or birth control?

Who wants the inconvenience of gunk in our bodies? Gooey nasty gunk that might take on the traits of either donor which might be corrupted into a useful life is no way to go if one is not ready. How do we answer this plague of society that women suffer year after year. Not abortion, I mean pregnancy. Do we forget that we were once this nasty gunk ourselves?

Is a fetus more like cancer, enlarging and spreading throughout the abdomen until it begins to think for itself, feels pain, hears music and voices only to be born to a life as a representative in congress that favors the cause that no more like him or her will ever exist again? Horrors! The gunk might evolve into a Right Wing Christian or even a mother itself!

Yes, the gunk must be destroyed for the good of society before it is loved, before it is recognized as a human being where is might be cherished, fed and nourished. OOOOO! The horror! The terror!

A woman will not have to say "I had an abortion." But instead she can say "I had a fetus and my doctor took care of it. I feel much better now." Why not tell children of the ravages of abortion and the benefits of marriage? Life is not a magical mystery tour of trial and error. The trials and errors of past generations are well documented for all to see. The old adage that if you do not learn from history you will surely repeat its mistakes is true. Arrogance is the father of destruction.

Let us not have any fantasy on the merit of abortion. What parent would take his/her child and crush their head in a vise? Would you not be attached to that child even two hours after he/she was born? What parent would take their child and him/her in the middle of a freeway to fend for themselves? What sane person would condone or demand the killing of one's own child? How can there be those who fight for the rights of children ignore the destruction of millions of children? You hear politicians and teachers speak about the welfare of children to get elected, and favor abortion.

In the same light, politicians care about social security, but try to pass laws for euthanasia. Interestingly they save social security yet will use euthanasia to keep costs down.

How does any politician stand waist deep in aborted babies and say 'This is where I stand. Vote for me, vote for life.' Lack of common sense is when you hand a condom to a child believing he will not use it as a balloon.

Let us ignore "Thou shalt not kill" as well as other verses concerning the killing of the innocent. In the case of abortion how dare God tell us what to do with our bodies? Let the courts decide on the issue until common sense prevails and it is again outlawed. Now for the courts to decide how the moral issue must be solved brings that decision back to the Bible. To argue the case we must discuss the issue of morality which leads us to the writer of the Bible. Wait a minute, that's not possible because then we would have to accept the existence of God in order to take Him to court. So, first, we must bring evidence that proves He exists both in written testimony and witnesses to the fact. With separation of Church and State all written works based on His existence might be construed as advancing a view of a governmentally accepted religion.

Another problem is that God has no assets to take if a civil case is leveled at Him. However, the churches represent God so we would be justified to take them to court to satisfy any financial obligations. Wait a minute, if we bring in the churches they will testify to the before mentioned information of scripture which could bias the outcome of the case.

So how do we argue the problem of infanticide? Sorry. Abortion? For God has a problem with the moral issue of abortion. Is not abortion the taking of innocent human life after conception? How can one argue differently unless one's moral compass does not always point north? Do fetuses not bleed? Not feel? Are without a soul?

What about quality of life or the life of the mother? If the fetus is deformed or horribly afflicted wouldn't we be doing a kindness by ripping it out of the afflicted mother's womb? Sorry, surgically removed it by the loving hands of the abortionist and his nurse, then gently place into a trash bag for ready disposal and oblivion? Society and the family are in win-win situations because the family suffers less financially and emotionally sans fetus because it would be a terrible thing for a fetus to be forced to live and breathe anywhere near us.

What of the life of the mother? Medical science has advanced far enough to save both mother and child. If there are complications then nature has spoken not a medical procedure.

Planned Parenthood came out with interesting statistics a few years back detailing the reasons for abortion. They are as follows:

Oh yeah, I forgot, any reason will do to kill children.

Supposedly, there are gray areas that God neither considers nor understands. God only thinks in black and white, but does that mean He is racially motivated? Should we make God the political pawn in the way He thinks? Maybe I should have said He thinks in right or wrong, but isn't right or wrong relative to the age in which we live in?

God does think in terms of right or wrong. He tells us this in scripture. Gray areas are human frailty issues. When we sit on a fence and say we can not decide where to stand on such issues then we must be reminded of:

"You are neither hot nor cold and I will spew you out of my mouth"

Rev. 3:15

Man thinks in terms of selfishness, political convenience, arrogance, cowardice, and moral apologetics.

When is life not a life? Is conception inorganic assimilation of cells accidentally forming into a fetus or is it the beginning of a violent struggle to stay in the womb from the ravages of the outside world? Common sense tells you it is the beginning of life, but political agendas tell us it is a confusing process that only a law can explain without moral definition. However, scientific explanations only confuse the issue and religious explanations only infuriate those who wish to keep it between us mortals.

If the mass of flesh has hands like a child, feels pain like a child, has a nose, mouth and ears of a child, it is not a duck, but a child. It is politically incorrect to talk of the horrors of abortion, but alright to express the benefits after the procedure.

There are enough empty spaces, empty chairs where children should be laughing, learning and being loved. Are there not enough Cherubim and Seraphim above us that we need to add to their numbers? There is no reason to believe that anything good comes from a society that sacrifices children for individual freedom of an unclear choice. It is only unclear to those who reason that be using this choice they will gain socially and politically. Do we worship the god Uranus who ate his own children? Do we follow the ancients who sacrifice children for the gods of rock and lava? Are we not progressing to genetically engineered children so they will not be physically challenged, age challenged, spiritually challenged or politically challenged?

When unborn children become trash or science experiments, what does that tell us about a society? Hundreds of thousands of Cambodians were massacred in the 1980's and we were outraged for a few moments. World War II had millions of Jews and Christians killed in concentration camps which horrified everyone except those who say it never happened. Saddam Hussein tortured and murdered thousands of his own countrymen, yet when we freed them many cried out that the Iraqi's were better off under his rule. How long before we say that the second holocaust of abortion is just as terrifying and why we did nothing? Are we not barbarians, too? Do we think so little of life as the Cambodian leaders, the Nazi regime, or Hussein's insane demagoguery? What will be our aftermath?

If God thinks it is life's beginnings, then the religious debate starts concerning whose God do we think is speaking? Does God exist? And if so who is He to judge us since we have free will to kill anything we want? Is God a metaphor? Spirit? Deep consciousness? A moral pause before an action is taken? Or is God a symbol for man's yearning for an explanation for His own sad existence?

God can not be proved, analyzed, or physically touched so He must be a psychotic break in man's psyche over his moral breach and inhumanity to itself. Man can not bring himself to say to this God that II Chronicles 7: 14 is too simple to change this world:

"If my people, who are called by My name, will humble themselves and pray and seek My face and turn from their wicked ways, then will I hear from heaven and will forgive their sin and will heal their land."

Humble ourselves? Never! Are we not arrogant to think we can only fix things by ourselves? It's too easy, so we will continue to try and pass laws allowing the unborn to continue to die. Let us ignore the fact that death is the only outcome of abortion. Ignore the psychological trauma that women suffer from regret and guilt from abortion. Ignore the fact that father's-to-be breathe a sigh of relief for not having to raise the child or marrying a woman they do not love. Ignore the fact that any society which vicariously kill their offspring do not honor life, God or themselves. If life is not held dear, then our freedoms and way of life shall surely vanish from the face of the earth.

Our answer to the problem of abortion is to educate our children in a different way then sex classes in schools that encourage sexual experimentation. In schools students are taught sex is great, but don't try it without a condom or some form of contraception. The theory is that children will experience sex anyway so why not protect themselves? A better theory is to tell them the ravages of abortion, the guilt of multiple partners that denigrates the sanctity of marriage and show the advantage of a permanent relationship in marriage. Multiple partners bring about unwanted pregnancies. Unwanted pregnancies bring about abortion or out of wedlock births. Those children born out of wedlock are blamed for unhappiness and poverty of single women. Poverty brings government assistance putting burdens on taxpayer's wallets with higher taxes. Higher taxes bring about societal hardships on all families. At the end of the finger pointing society looks upward and shakes its collective fist at God and says "How can you let this happen?"

How dare God tell us what to do? The cycle is complete. We do not want to believe in God therefore it is God's fault we are suffering. The rationale of human beings is that we want to walk our own life, yet we want to know there is something greater than ourselves somewhere out there. However, we do not want to be responsible for our actions and if God exists, we will have to act accordingly. What is free will if we are forced to make the right decision despite our temerity to do otherwise. Free will is action of thinking human beings to do right or wrong, but the consequences are defined by the choices we make. God tells us that we can choose to accept Him or reject Him, but with that choice He has the option to accept or reject you when you stand before Him. Life is not a magical mystery trip of trial and error. The trials and errors of past generations are well documented for all to see. The old adage that if you do not learn from history, you will surely repeat its mistake is true. Arrogance is the father of destruction.

God not need be thought of as a cosmic belch. Likewise, let us not have any fantasy on the merits of abortion. What parent would take his/her child and crush their head in a vise? Would you not be attached to that child even two hours after he/she was born? What parent would take their child and leave him/her in the middle of a freeway to fend for himself/herself? What sane person would condone or demand the killing of another child? How can there be those who fight for the rights of children and ignore the destruction of millions of children?

All our decisions have become politically motivated where the end is power over the individual. One day we will all hear the cries of the unborn and no amount of tears will silence them.

CHAPTER ELEVEN

Rap Star

I used to be someone's superstar
Now I can't see quite quite that far
The world was mine to set you free
Now it looks like a yo-yo-Me
What other God comes to stand and talk
Get out of my way where I walk
Cause I'm hip, I'm hip.
I'm hip, I'm hip.
I'm hip hop hip hop hip
Now Easter Bunny has nothing on me
No way he'll ever set you free
Don't get the feeling I'm a real dead stiff
For you're in for a surprise cause if, if
I said if I did not rise from the grave
What monkey will come for you to save?
Uh-huh, uh-huh, uh-huh, uh-huh.
Cause I'm hip, I'm hip
I'm hip hop hip hop hip
On the Cross I died for you
It is what it is do you believe it's true?
I give eternal life just for free
Who you goin' believe now them or Me?
I'm the One you come to meet
So don't go thinking this is a two way street.

Cause I'm hip
I'm hip hop hip hop hip
I did not come to this world so sad
I came to you to make you glad
What reason would you have to turn your
back
Unless it's because you're an old sad sack
I won't come again unless the Word is told
So don't be silent with your lips stone cold
Cause I'm hip
I'm hip hop hip hop hip.

If Jesus came today would He have
been a rap singer to reach the young people
of our age? Let's move to a more extreme
question, Can you imagine Christian suicide
bombers? If that is the greatest sacrifice for
your faith why are we not impressed by such
dedication? Being persecuted for your faith
is another matter. If you die because you
will not renounce your faith in Christ under
duress then that is the ultimate sacrifice.

Non-Christians can not stand to hear
your testimony and see that you believe it.
The words bring guilt and emptiness to their
own lives. So it is important to bring down
the perfection of Christ by bringing out your

imperfections. So when you lie, cheat, curse or steal in a moment of weakness the non-believer will jump on you for the rest of your life for that one weakness. If you sin, their relief is that God does not exist, God is not all-powerful, God is not to be trusted because you have not shown them the perfection they are seeking. We are not here to be perfect, but bring our imperfection to Christ. Our testimony is that though we still sin, we are forgiven. Our perfection is in our ascension to Heaven when this life is over. We can not allow those who do not believe to be a virus that brings doubt to the race we run.

CHAPTER TWELVE

Love thy neighbor, turn the other cheek, forgive your enemies.

Danger! Danger! The Christians are coming! The Christians are coming!

If God were one of us, He would be considered a narrow-minded intolerant right-wing religious bigot. How do we draw that conclusion? From our Lord's own words:

"I will have no other gods before me…" Intolerant towards other religions.

"No one who is a murderer…enter the kingdom of heaven." Bigotry, intolerance.

"I am the way the truth and the life… Egotist, self-righteous.

Where is the tolerance for everyone? The gates of heaven should be open to all no matter what they believe. Isn't that so? Not! Why can't we as Christians petition the Lord our God into changing His ways instead of the other way around? Acceptance of all things of man and turning the other cheek is that not being a fool for Christ? Being a fool for Christ does not mean being a fool in spite of Christ. What manner of evil calls for God to come down from heaven and compromise His perfection in judgment and spirit?

God Himself came down to save us and our gratitude is, at best, questionable. We want to live forever, but only on our terms. We want to enter Heaven, but only by the road we choose. We want to be successful, but the power and money that is involved only puts God in a dark closet that we dare not enter. When we are in desperate need we pray on our knees. When that need is met we continue running from our obligation and gratefulness to Him who saved us. We rationalize the blessings and decide it would have happened anyway so we never soil our knees again.

What is the beauty of the passion of Christ? Is it one life for all lives? Is it the vicious beating from the Romans? Betrayal of the Jews? Is it the finger pointing between Jews and Gentiles? Is it the tears of blood in prayer? Is it the sound of the nails pounding into the calloused flesh? Where is the beauty?

The passion of Christ was the world itself trying to obliterate our only chance of eternal survival. The passion of Christ goes on today with many trying to quell their guilt and lust by crying out "There is no God!" To repeat the lie that there is no God is the hope that it becomes truth. What person in any right mind would hope for such a thing? The deafening cries of

"Crucify Him! Crucify Him!" still echo in every corner of the world. Sadly, the church is starting to whisper the same words. What have we become where the truth is questioned because the lies are branded on the foreheads of those around us?

A gun is pointed at our heads, a threat of death is offered in the words "Who do you serve?" and the trigger is pulled for the wrong answer. That answer is "I serve the Lord."

Christianity is an archaic faith not to be trusted, but vilified because of its teaching of unrealistic morality and ethical behavior. However, Islam is relevant because it is physically dangerous. It is easier to ignore God, but not the sword over our heads. For some odd reason Christians are not the good guys. We want you to live forever, Islam wants us to die forever or betray our own convictions. Where is the reason for this? What happens to the commandment 'Thou shalt not kill'? The Koran encourages violence to get conversions which, if it were a life changing religion, we would willingly beat down the doors to convert.

Christians say we must save the infidels. No other religion compares to Christianity because of the Scripture:

"I am the way, the truth, and the life. No one comes to the Father except through Me."   John 14:6

If you find that statement intolerant to all other religions, then it is. It is intolerance to blasphemy, political correctness, mediocre commitment to God, sexual deviancy, and illiterate interpretations.

Blasphemy where those who say they believe say Jesus is not the Son of God, that He did not die on the cross, that he married a prostitute, that He was only a prophet, only a good man, a charlatan, a magician, a heretic and did not rise from the dead.

Political correctness where issues of abortion, euthanasia, liberalism, socialism, excessive taxation, homosexuality, war, poverty, racism, and political crime are excused with a shrug and nervous laughter.

Mediocre commitment to God where going to church on Sunday is enough then fearing to speak of Him the other six days when confronted, giving silent denial while the cock crows three times and excusing yourself from prayer during meals are signs of intolerance to God. What are you thinking when others watch you for signs of divine intervention in your life and see none forthcoming?

Sexual deviancy where gay marriage, multi-sexual partners, and premarital sex are overlooked in the name of love. Perversion supersedes conversion because the content causes the inner sinful curiousness of man to want to look, yet not look at the perversion.

Cowardice where fear of allowing others to know we follow Christ, fear of standing alone, if necessary, against those who curse our Lord and fear of not being able to quote scripture to change discussions or defend the faith makes cowards of us all.

Illiterate interpretations where revisionist scripture that fits politically correct discussions and to excuse morally reprehensible acts of society that common sense tells you are wrong are only excuses that must be made for social expediency. Is homosexuality acceptable because Christ does not speak of it directly? Christ did not speak of abortion so is that acceptable, too? Christ did not speak of euthanasia so we are ethically and morally right to put down our fathers and mothers?

When do we begin to use common sense that Jesus did not speak of these things because it was understood by those who read the scriptures that it was wrong? Why would He state the obvious to those who knew the scriptures unlike those of us today?

Must we tolerate the temper tantrums from those who want to do whatever makes them feel good whether it is drugs, alcohol, sex or gambling. Confusion over religion comes from the fact that Christianity has no unity, no sparks of faith that inspire. Pastors are held hostage in the pulpits from congregations that dictate procedures, content, and interpretations. Gossip and innuendoes destroy unwanted ministries that challenge the social norm. Chaos in the pulpits can not bring unity or draw the Spirit of God within its members. Some congregations believe it is their duty to meet our spiritual indulgences according to various levels of income. The greater the income the more blessings by the congregation they will receive.

Political gagging of the pulpit is backed by the repeal of tax exemptions which is vicariously invoked depending on whether you are Republican or Democrat. Our forefathers would have scoffed at such a threat and continued on. Did they not speak against taxation and King George despite the threats? Our freedom to speak is a narrow right to speak our mind.

The division of the churches has wreaked havoc in the spiritual lives and intelligent design of our future. The Catholic Church has suffered greatly over the child molestation cases, but Catholics have returned to their parishes. What would make them do such a thing? Are their priests not perverts, criminals and sinners? The media furiously tried to bring down the Catholic Church, but Catholics refuse to abandon their God.

The Anglican and Episcopal churches are fighting gay priests and bishops which are tearing apart their congregations. Shaking their fists at God these individuals tell us that they are special, that their homosexuality is a gift from God which makes no sense at all when scripture speaks against it:

"Do you not know that the wicked will not inherit the kingdom
of God? Do not be deceived: Neither the sexual immoral nor
idolaters nor adulterers nor male prostitutes nor homosexual
offenders....will inherit the kingdom of God."
I Corinthians 6: 9

How do we unite all churches without turning them into an ecumenical stew that includes paganism, atheism, Islam, Buddhism, Taoism, the Occult and all other minor faiths, beliefs, and mythology? We divide ourselves by identifying ourselves as Baptists, Catholics, Presbyterians, and Unitarians, etc, etc. We are Christians, yet we want to be unique in our identification.

How do we differentiate from others who are dying for the souls of the world? We do this for the sake of Christ which other faiths do not. Jehovah Witnesses are not witnesses for Christ. Mormons are not witnesses for Christ. Moonies are not witnesses for Christ. Any faith that does not put Christ as the center for redemption of sins and the goal of everlasting life with God is not a true Christian faith.

Since when are real Christians a danger to society? Since when have Christians been suspect for political positions? Since when are real Christians a danger to the judiciary? Why can't Christians run industry? Since when should we hide in closets as if we are source of evil? What walls are we hide behind to keep our light from the rest of society? If we are to be the salt of the earth and not the artificial sweetener, to stir within the mortal immortality and peace to the chaos of this world, then we must tell others that the path of Christ does not lead into a mysterious maze, but a narrow road that is straight and right to a definite end.

Do we pray not expecting an answer? For how fearsome is prayer if God listens to our words? Prayer is not a series of numbers and gibberish that many call prayer language. God is not an author of confusion so why do we try to confuse Him with a supposed gift that has no interpretation? The object of prayer language is to draw attention to the speaker and make it easier to lack commitment for any given issue.

Do not blurt out something to impress those around you for the silence afterwards without interpretation sends the message of confusion. If you are insulted by that comment, good. We need to speak clearly of God's love, faith, blessing and sacrifice for the world to understand that our God is an awesome God.

"For God is not a God of disorder but of peace."

I

Corinthians 14: 33

Throughout history we honored those who stood up and fought the fight for our freedoms. Many paid with their lives in the American Revolution, WWI, WWII and now in Iraq and Afghanistan. We have made legends around diverse individuals such as George Washington, Davy Crockett, Jim

Bowie, Abraham Lincoln and many, many more. Now we humanize them into fallible weaker asterisks of history. We demonize the faith of our fathers into trivial pursuit answers in an exaggerated game.

In each new conflict great men appeared to take up the gauntlet for freedom and faith. Names such as Andrew Jackson in the War of 1812, George Washington in the Revolutionary War, Crockett and Bowie at the Alamo, Pershing in WWI, Patton in WWI and Reagan during the Cold War are names that history reveres.

Now the religious world and political arena we have Martin Luther, Calvin, Watts, Wesley, Martin Luther King Jr. and many others. Recently we have Billy Graham, Dr. James Dobson, Dr. James Kennedy to name a few. Yet, who will stand when they are gone? What names come to mind that will be the conscious of this nation? Who is our next Washington, Lincoln or Roosevelt? Who will be out next Patton, Lee, Grant or Pershing? Who will be our next Edison, Einstein or Ford. Who will be our next Luther, Calvin or Wesley?

We have become the generation that has destroyed our heroes and speak gibberish to our God. No hero or leader is perfect, but God is. When confronted with perfection, in this case God Almighty, we refuse to accept perfection. We are not a godless nation, but a guilty country trying to hide our guilt.

We want to trample those we perceive to be better than we are. We want perfection in imperfection because we need to know it is an unattainable goal. We want it to be unattainable so we don't strain ourselves in our sin, rather we want to wallow in our sins as pigs in a muddy sty. We cannot stand to feel guilty, cannot understand the perfection we seek and cannot accept our own imperfection. We live in turmoil and jealous rage over others who have come to Christ and revel in their destruction. Our immortality looks filthy in the daylight of Heaven as we look for shade to hide ourselves from His sight.

We have hung a sign on our Bibles that read 'Do not disturb." We pray while sleeping in our pews with one eye open and our minds drifting over images miles away. It is then we wonder why our prayers are not answered.

God must be asking "What is your question? I only hear a maze of mumbling echoes. What you say and what your mind reveals to Me are a contradiction." We say "But we pray to You so do something! Why won't you listen to us?" God answers us and says "As you pray you think of sinful things.

As you pray you dream of adultery. As you pray you show anger against others. As you pray you yearn for fame and fortune. As you pray you become deaf to My words. As you pray you speak only of you."

We ask "What shall we do then?" God says "Learn first if I am truly your God or if you are your own god. Learn next that I do not accept a grocery list of convenience. I am not a horn of plenty spilling out riches and success for a fee of tithes and offerings. Accept nothing and expect everything. I am not here to obey your every whim. I am not here just to ease your guilty conscious from day to day. Confession is good for the soul, but it not payment for continuous sinning. I am here as your God so that you will follow and worship Me. Then I will bless you as I see fit, not as you demand."

And God continues to speak: "I judge you and you will not judge Me. I am Alpha and Omega and you are the iota in the alphabet of life. Without Me you have no meaning. Without Me you are finite and dust. Without Me you are worthless as coal before it is shaped into a diamond. Without Me you waste your breath with meaningless words and empty gestures. Without Me there is no church, no chance of peace, no hope of resurrection and no reason to strive for the good of humanity. If I lift My hand from this world, it will be no more. Not because I will it, but as you will it."

If you can believe that, then it is true "The Christians are coming, the Christians are coming!"

CHAPTER THIRTEEN
Conversation One

Narrator: "Welcome to Meet Your Maker. Meet Your Maker is supported by the Heavenly Host and Angelic Foundation for the Preservation of St. Peter's Gate. Today's guest is I. M. Running. Mr. Running is a six term Senator of the United States and head of two Senate committees. I.M. Running is in the hot seat, excuse the expression, with our Host, God."

(Host of Heaven applaud long and loud)

God: "My guest today is I. M. Running who will be defending his views and actions over the past 68 years. Welcome Mr. Running."

Running: "Thank you, sir. I am delighted to be here."

God: "We'll see. My first question is for you to tell us about yourself, your faith and your personal history. We do have it on replay, but I would like to hear it from you."

Running: "I go to the All-Purpose Righteous Church every chance I get. It's difficult to go every Sunday when you're running for office."

God: "You're not the only one who does that. Why should you enter here is what we are discussing."

Running: "I have a loving wife who adores me and I adore her. We have three beautiful children and a dog named Matrix."

God: "Then your three months of therapy worked? Your wife is no longer seeing your best friend, your eldest son has finished drug rehabilitation, and your teenage daughter has decided to keep her child? By the way, it's a boy. It is difficult when your wife is thirty years younger than you and your other two wives want so much from you financially and emotionally it is difficult to keep the present family together."

Running(slowly): Yes, that's all behind us. My younger son is very active in the church."

God: "Yes, I know, I've heard from him. However, back to you. Do you think your past will hurt your election here?

Running: "My constituency is very forgiving."

God: "That depends."

Running: "For myself, I changed a great deal over the last year. All these problems have made me realize what I have lost and gained. I want your viewers to look at me and know I am a different person now."

God: "I have no viewers of this program. It is only me and you. I am always here."

(Chorus singing in the background with hand clapping)

Running: "I thought I heard applause...."

God: "Automatic adoration, real as it is, it's to be expected."

Running: "Oh."

God: "Let's hear your platform to convince me why you ran for Congress."

Running: "I am for the people." (waits for applause, hears none)

God: "Then you intended to meet the needs of everyone in your district and state?"

Running: "Well, no one could meet everyone's needs."

God: "I can. Answer my question."

Running: "I have committed myself to my faith."

God: "When was that?"

Running: "December, 1976."

God: "And to whom did you commit this faith?"

Running: "My church...before the congregation, of course."

God: "You remember it better than I."

Running: (frustrated) "I gave generously to my church."

God: "And for that they made you a Trustee."

Running: (proudly) "In good standing, yes, and I did charity work."

God: "Which helped you get into office."

Running: "I am faithful to my wife, too."

God: "Is that your first wife or your second, perhaps your third??"

Running: "I had no allegiance to you until after my second wife and that is the truth."

God: "Oh?"

Running: "I have not lied to my constituency."

God: "Not once?"

Running: "Embellishing to save hurt feelings is not lying."

God: "I see."

Running: "If you compare my record with my colleagues, you will see my terms in office outshine theirs."

God: "Water frozen over mud also shines brightly, but does not hide the mud. I am not part of your constituency so trying to convince me if you were the less of many evils does not merit brownie points."

Running: "How am I doing so far?"

God: "Let's take a poll."
Silence all around.
Running: "You must have only Republicans up here."
God: "We are not political here."
Running: "Then why am I here?"
God: "More of a formality."
Running: "Are we done yet?"
God: "This is not an election."
Running: "Can I ask you something?"
God: "Always;"
Running: "Are there any famous people here?"
God: "A few."
Running: "Is Confucius here?"
God: "No."
Running: "Is Mohammed here?"
God: "Who?"
Running: "How about philosophers like Nietzsche?"
God: "He's dead."
Running: "Socrates?"
God: "Sorry, no."
Running: "Any of them?"
God: "One or two."
Running: "What about politicians?"
God: "Depended on how they voted."
Running: "You're being evasive."
God: "We're here to talk about you."
Running: "Then I ask again, why am I here?"

God: "To convince me why I should let you in."

Running: "I have voted for several bills in the Senate to outlaw abortion and put restrictions on euthanasia. I am seen in church most Sunday's. I celebrate Easter and Christmas with my family. I have mentioned you a number of times with friends and colleagues. What more would you ask of me?"

God: "You voted for those bills to pacify your constituency and knew full well they would not pass. You have said privately that you support abortion, euthanasia, and gay marriage. You are seen in church to hedge all bets that I may or may not exist. Got you there. You celebrate Easter and Christmas with your family, but very seldom at any other time of the year. You mentioned My holy name with your friends and colleagues in passing to get their influence and vote. I ask more from you than what you can give which is less than what you have. I am the Lord your God. You neither tremble nor kneel in My presence. You show no respect and talk to Me as if we are familiar with each other's company. I do not know you well enough to allow you to spend eternity since you are neither warm nor cold, but lukewarm."

Running: "I am politically correct. It is a matter of debate on other issues."

God: "I am not politically correct and it is not debatable."

Running: "I accept the necessity of a woman's right to choose."

God: "Choose what?"

Running: "Whether to risk her life for the inconvenience of a family which would deprive her of the lifestyle she is used to."

God: "What lifestyle would that be?"

Running: "The pursuit of happiness, to attain goals of financial freedom, to be unhindered by society's moral objection."

God: "In other words sexual immorality and selfishness. What of the unborn?"

Running: "Science has made great strides in stem cell research...."

God: (visibly angry) "What of the child?"

Running: "It is a fact of life in our society that certain choices have casualties..."

God: "But what of the child!" The voice of God echoed throughout the heavens.

Running: "Obviously, sir, you are pro-life. Can we go on to something else?"

God: "What about euthanasia?"

Running: "You're tough, sir. I believe in the right to die…"

God: "You mean suicide or murder."

Running: "Sir, you are making it difficult…There are individual rights and issues to be addressed here. The need for compassion towards those who suffer so much."

God: "You have decided to treat their pain with death?"

Running: "I am not a physician, but research has shown us that it would be best to ease their pain."

God: "You look like you are in pain. Would you like me to ease that pain?"

Running: "No, No, I'm fine. Thank you. That judgment is not mine to make at this time."

God: "No, it's mine."

Running: "Then where's the compassion, the love…the..the

God: "The forgiveness?"

Running: "Yes, forgiveness!"

God: "It is left at the gates when My World is ignored, My passion is mocked, and My forgiveness is never asked for till you stand here before Me.

Running: "Surely this is not what you want for those unfortunate….

God: "It was their decision and don't call me Shirley.

Running: "Old joke, sir.

God: "It was to show you I have a sense of humor, but not concerning those who turn their back on Me.

Running: "I approve of separation of church and state for the good of both."

God: "Without Me there is no such thing as a good state, only moral decay."

Running: "Then we would have a theocracy."

God: "No, you would have a moral state with common sense and justice for all."

Running: "Concessions must be made for the greater good."

God: "Concession is a weakness in those who have no backbone to decide between right or wrong."

Running: "The rules change with each generation. We have to change with them."

God: "I helped write a book about that."

Running: "Yeah, right, but we were left with a lot of questions."

God: "Not on my part."

Running: "What is it you want me to know then?"

God: "I am."

Running: "You are what, sir?"

God: "Wrong answer."

Running: "I am trying to give you the appropriate response, sir."

God: "It's not working."

Running: "I did not ask to come here."

God: "I know that."

Running: "If there are no more questions, may I continue my political career?"

God: "That's not possible."

Running: "Why?"

God: "You're dead."

Running: I've seen my polls. No, sir, I'm leading by six points!

God: "My polls tell me you've lost by a landslide.

Running: "Are we through then?"

God: "Yes."

Running: "How do I get out of here? I have an election to run."

God: "The elevator or the stairs are available to you, but they only go down."

Running: "Great! I have two bills in Congress pending, two unfinished books I'm writing, and now you're sending me downstairs. No negotiation, no retrial. Do you have a phone?"

God: "I have direct dial, but there is a pay phone at the bottom of the stairs."

Running: "Got any change?"

God: "Sorry, no."

(Overhead speaker): Welcome to Meet Your Maker! Our next guest is U.R.

Mine, missionary to Central Africa, doctor and pastor to hundreds of those with A.I.D.S., cancer and starvation....

As Running climbs down the stairs the voices trail off, then a thunderous ovation and song erupt above him.

CHAPTER FOURTEEN
Conversation 2

Terrorist: "Welcome to Conversion to Islam 101. Two things you must have in this class is the Koran and a sword. We encourage group interaction. We have many guests here today and they have been volunteered to be examples for our class. First is this man whom is apparent that he comes from the Great Satan United States. Ah, what faith are you?"

Man in jeans: "I am a Christian."

Terrorist: "Very good. Now class this is the only and most important question to ask this infidel. Will you denounce your faith and convert to the holy word of the Koran and Islam?"

Man in jeans: "I am sorry, I can not."

Terrorist: "Very good answer. So you refuse?"

Man in jeans: "I must refuse."

Terrorist: (cuts off the man's head) "Go with Christ! Allah is great! Next!

Man in a brown robe: "Yes?"

Terrorist: "What is your religion?"

Man in a brown robe: "I am a Buddhist."

Terrorist: "Good! Good! Ah, you believe in reincarnation do you not?"

Man in a brown robe: "It depends on how one lives one's life."

Terrorist: "Now class the same question. Will you convert to Islam and kiss the book of the Koran?"

Man in brown robe: "I can not."

Terrorist: "Good! I wish to see what you will become in the next life. (cuts off his head)

Second terrorist slaps his arm as a mosquito bites him.

Terrorist: "So much for that next life. I wonder what will be next? A fly perhaps? Next!"

Man in a suit: "Yes?"

Terrorist: "What faith are you?"

Man in suit: "I am a Jehovah Witness."

Terrorist: "I understand you have trouble with dates when it comes to the end of the world."

Jehovah Witness: "Like you I believe that Jesus was a prophet and not divine. The end of the world will come soon enough.

Terrorist: "I did not ask you that. You do believe the Pope is the Anti-Christ, so do we. Yet, we demand you convert to Islam!"

Jehovah Witness: "I can not."

Terrorist: (cuts off his head) "Aw, nuts, I wanted to ask about getting off their mailing list. Next!"

A Jew walks in. Terrorist cuts off his head without even asking the question.

Terrorist: "I already knew his answer. Next!"

A liberal socialist walks in.

Terrorist: "My friend, you may pass. Say hello to my friends in Congress. Next! Who are you?"

Me: "I am ecumenical man for my great grandfather was Jewish, my mother was Presbyterian and my father was Catholic. I am a Jewlicaterian and ecumenical man. I can leap tall buildings at a single bound, but I choose not to for I have a fear of heights. I am faster spiritually than a speeding bullet only if that bullet is thrown instead of shot. I am disguised as a retail salesman because I do not wish to alarm my customers for I am ecumenical man!"

Terrorist: "All I heard was your great grandfather was a Jew.

Me: "I said I was ecumenical man."

Terrorist: "That's silly. I think I'll slap you on the side of the head with the flat of my sword. Then I'll throw you out of my class."

Absurd? To a point, but it is the danger we face in a world where we ignore the danger of a religious war where ignorance will be our own destruction. The danger is blind faith within the lunacy of any religion that tries to convert by force. It is a must that we believe God is in control in all things or we will lose all hope.

CHAPTER FIFTEEN

*Confession has absolution only when
repentance, not repetition, is absolute.*

Is it more exciting and fulfilling to commit the sin or to be told you are forgiven for that sin? If you are told to go and sin no more, do you believe that it is a moment of redemption or relief? Redemption from the guilt of the sin or relief so you can commit it again? We are sin junkies looking for the church to remove the guilt of sin week after week without the burden of regret. God is a drive-thru guru to make us feel good and not someone to justify our actions.

Why read scripture when the video takes less time to experience? Why become missionaries when it is easier to support someone else to be a missionary? We do not want to be challenged because we no longer have the urgency to believe. If this is not true then why is our nation rolling blindly down a steep hill? If our government and society are becoming more corrupt, then why are we silent?

What is it you want to say to God as a Christian? That our Lord Jesus Christ suffered and died for us, rose again so we might rise later with Him and it is not enough? Do we expect to be all King's kids whereby we exert our spiritual prowess based on wealth, power and prestige? And if we do not have any of these fine attributes, have we failed in our Christian walk? Many Christians are poor, many Christians do not have a voice in their church or community and many Christians are not respected for their needs for daily living relying on God to get through unscathed. Unscathed in sin, blessed with small blessings, and few kind words from out of the void of that part of society that looks down upon them.

The modern Church looks upon a poor man as spiritually lacking in faith and blessings. Everyone is not financially successful or powerful. The church expects pillars of society, but the disciples were killed by pillars of society. Should we base spiritual success in terms of money, property or political power?

Many members of churches do not want to grow up spiritually because it means being vulnerable to the wolves unleashed in society. We want to reinterpret the old adage when I was a child I spoke as a child, played like a child and thought like a child. When I grew up not a thing changed. It is unbiblical if you are a Christian, but we find security in childish things. We find excuses in child-like thoughts because we fear growing old, dying and meeting our Maker.

Some embrace Humanism who think God is a threat to our freedom. Believing in God is an embarrassment, sometimes even to Christians. Simple phrases such as God loves you, Jesus loves you brands one as an ultra right wing fanatic to be avoided at all costs and watched as a threat to freedom and social order. To believe in God and Jesus Christ makes you bereft of reality, unable to make sane decisions.

To be a Christian you should not hold office, vilified if you seek to be a Supreme Court Justice, a CEO in a company such as Chick-fil-A or President of the United States. To be a Christian you are a demon against freedom, patriotism and the democratic process. The problem with non-Christians, anti-God militants is that they attack the Creator and the sinner. A sinner's past is suspect and easier to attack than God and scripture. When the faith cannot dissect the man must be put on the table.

Eat, drink and be merry you may die or eat, drink and be merry and you will surely die. What is there to grasp and understand here? Do you want to party now without God or party later with God? In Heaven God is the designated driver when you get drunk in the Spirit.

CHAPTER SIXTEEN
The world is a political zoo

The world is a political zoo with the following animals on the world stage for all to see:

1) Yeahbuts- Creatures that hear the truth and answer "Yeah, but…"
2) Whatifadons- Hairy bulky elephants that cannot accept facts or the truth of any issue not their own. When confronted with an absolute truth or absolute lie answer with "What if this happens or that happens?"
3) Sleeponitasaurus- These creatures of procrastination speak after an issue or decision has been made with "Let us wait and see for a few days, take a poll and understand how it will affect our lives so let us sleep on it." Never mind whether it is right or wrong.
4) Thickskulldathons- Creatures that cannot hear or see the truth because it relentlessly bangs its head against the wall and then puts sealing wax in its ears while

dancing in circles yelling "It cannot be true! It cannot be true!"

5) Classwarfareidyle- Winged, leather-skinned, underfed bat that truly believes the rich are the enemies of the poor and must be taxed into oblivion so that everyone can be poor.

6) Whatacrocadile- Creature that follows and listens to economists saying that less taxes equals more spending by consumers than roam past public domains repeating "What a crock!" to anyone who will listen.

The zoo is immense and the creatures endless.

CHAPTER SEVENTEEN
What will I Learn If Learning
Has No Education

In our schools the view of education is to teach the up-to-the minute reality of life. So we teach sexual education, political correctness and assorted intangibles instead of reading, writing, arithmetic, American History, science and social studies. Now social studies is interesting because it involves civics, the Constitution, early American History, basic economics and the power of the individual vote. However, that is not what modern education teaches and so we are stuck with the government we have now.

A few years ago, my neighbor told me that her daughter brought in pens, pencils, paper, notebooks and calculators to school. The teacher found that a couple of students could not afford the same things so she gathered up everyone's material and then redistributed equally all the things the parents bought for their children. That day she was taught the supposed value of socialism and her parents were taught the power that government can have on our lives.

Another example is that even today teachers cannot speak ill of terrorists and tone down teaching patriotism. If teachers speak of the Bible or try to teach Creationism they risk disciplinary action or being fired. The Ten Commandments is an abomination not only in schools, but in the courts. Political correctness has taught our children that our society is evil, our country is morally corrupt and our way of life is wrong. Professors in college mock God and the Bible informing their students that Christianity is an illusion. No conservative thinking is allowed unless you plan to fail the course. Yet, the Koran is studied with various other beliefs where man is the center of the universe. Deletions of historical fact are commonplace when it comes to the founding of this country.

Does the press believe it will only criticize Islamic terrorists if it overwhelms the world? Does the Church believe it will be able to offer an alternative to Islam or any other religion if the world is overwhelmed? Does the government think the Constitution would not be burned by those who wait for us to fall? The Trojan Horse is our public education and we refuse to think it is a danger to our freedom.

We are told if we criticize Islam, they will kill us when they get the chance. We teach our children to be less critical of Islam and more critical of Christianity which Islam hates. Which enemy would you rather have when it comes to education? A religion of death or a religion of life?

Jehovah Witnesses have called the Pope the Anti-Christ which is found in their Red Book I received from door to door visitations. Do you hear of death squads coming from the Vatican to punish them? We live in an Age of Ignorance. We are ignorant of the lessons of history. When Hitler was appeased he nearly destroyed all of Europe and Africa. We now appease North Korea, Iran and half the middle east which only re-avow their wish to destroy Israel and the United States. Islam preaches with a bloody sword and the Koran is their honing stone.

How much has been gained under Christianity in thought, inventions, science, free speech, free press, financial independence, and freedom even for the religion that wished to destroy us. Nothing has been ventured from Islam in 1100 years. What free thinkers have come out of the Middle East? Why is it not taught that true Christianity does not threaten your life for not believing. True Christianity tolerates evil and seeks to overcome to overcome it by faith and prayer in Christ. True Christianity has conversion by water and spirit instead of blood by the sword.

We cannot have Judeo-Christian moral values because Separation of Church and State brings the narrow-mindedness will not allow other lifestyles and moral codes. We are forced to find other means without a higher authority involved to enforce guilt and responsibility to make moral behavior and ethical standards work.

How is this a problem? Thirteen state constitutions have publically acknowledged Jesus Christ, the Declaration of Independence mentions the Creator, and the Constitution of the United States does not mention Separation of Church and State, but it is in the Russian Constitution.

The national media is fighting for a socialist state. Parts of our government push economic equality for the masses. However, pure socialism is where everyone is treated the same without a tyrannical hierarchy that dictates our way of life. Unfortunately, if we taught the historical background of socialism no one would dare pursue it. It never worked for Russia, China, the old iron curtain countries, South America and Latin America. Poverty and despair abound in these nations so why do we pursue this dangerous belief? Why then when socialism is defeated in these countries do the people celebrate? It is because they realize the freedom that they lost through ignorance is now found again. They find they can speak without imprisonment, free to earn a true living, free to worship and free to pursue happiness of their choosing.

Equality in human terms is not attainable, socialism in its purest form is unrealistic, democracy without a moral base, moral responsibility or moral conscious cannot be sustained. If we do not teach the downside of socialism then we are doomed to suffer the fate of its history which is total and abject failure.

This new education has failed as students kill other students (Virginia Tech), education scores are down, tests are revamped to give false scores, private schools are attacked and homeschoolers are the pariah of the NEA.

Vouchers are denounced by the NEA because it would tax money from public education. There would be no need of vouchers if public education taught the three R's, held moral responsibility high in its standards and dumped political correctness in confusing students with sexual ambiguity, political blinders, historical amnesia and religious persecution. Open mindedness is touted as long as it doesn't involve God, love of country and strict interpretation of the Constitution.

The hardest attack on education is the vilification of the Christian church which the elite believe is not a perfect option. They do not want it to be taught that God is in control instead of human beings. They do not believe God can bring about a perfect society where everyone is equal, everyone lacks want, everyone loves each other, no crime, no war, only peace and contentment. Humanistic socialism will never happen because we are flawed human beings who are never happy with whatever state or stage of life they are in.

There is no moral objective in the schools, not even an intellectual one for if we train our students to think for themselves they will make good, common sense choices in jobs, politics and lifestyles. The public school teaches equality in substandard information. Thomas Jefferson as overseer of education said that two books had to be taught in the public schools which were a hymnal and the Bible. Now it is not politically correct and an intolerant viewpoint. Education is governed by an even hand not the back of one.

How long will we sleep while the darkness covers us? Who will light the lantern to show the way from the edges of Armageddon? Will we hasten the Tribulation by our indifference in educating our children? Do we allow our leaders to brow beat them into making decisions that cost us our freedom? The rest of the world has closed in on us and Israel. Will we fall out of cowardice, indifference and our own petty greed? We cannot be defeated by armies, but we can be defeated financially because we want what we want. We can be defeated by the ignorance of short term education that denigrates our history, our vision and our national soul.

"But there were also false prophets among the people
    just as there will be false teachers among you. They
    will secretly introduce destructive heresies, even denying
    the sovereign Lord bought them
—bringing swift
    destruction on themselves."
2
Peter 2:1

Our public school systems teaches incompatibility of science and religion. Darwin vs. God. However science came into its own by devout Christians. Sir Isaac Newton wrote more on Theology than science. Many of the early scientists did not see a defining line between science and religion.

Where does this lead us? You cannot, you will not expunge the Word of God for the sake of public education. Russia tried it and failed. China tried it and failed. Most of the countries behind the old iron curtain failed to silence the Word of God. Hatred for Jesus Christ is irrational, ignorant of His coming and illogical passion for spiritual suicide. Jesus represents freedom to think, eternal life, redemption, peace, eternal love and satisfaction in the life one leads. No other religion has that for no other faith away from God can do the same. This does preclude the Jewish faith for our faith comes from the very God who is very God.

Our education basically teaches a me-me-me world. Life is too short, we are not rich enough, we are not happy in our relationships, our job, our free time, nothing satisfies is in that need to be recognized, loved and honored. Our children are taught that everything stinks in this world we live in because we are not the focus. With God and our Lord Jesus Christ the focus lies in two things, Him and us.

Once again "I am the Way..." Good people do not go to Heaven because they are good. "I am the Way...." Famous individuals do not go to Heaven because

they are famous. "I am the Truth…"
Relatives do not go to Heaven because you
loved them. "I am the Life…" This is not
cruel, but realistic in the reading of the
Scripture concerning Jesus Christ. You can
teach it as politically incorrect, unjust,
intolerant or bigoted, but it is God's Word
and promise.

CHAPTER EIGHTEEN
Wimpy Christianity

What kind of Christian would we be if Jesus listened to the Pharisees, Sadducees or Romans who told Him He was wrong? Would Jesus have said 'You're right and I'll get back to you on that. Let me call my Dad and see what He says, I mean, dying on the cross has got to hurt. So let me get back to you.'

So do we stand or cower in our faith? Do we reinterpret the scripture to justify our cowardice? Do we call our Dad in Heaven for redirection in His words? Or do we cry out to our Father in Heaven and say 'Here we stand, we can do no other!'
What are our differences with the rest of the world? Are they so vast they are beyond reconciliation? Let's see the list of changes made over the years to lessen the burden of our language:

Politically incorrect	Politically correct
Bible	Any other book
God	Spirit, Inner Essence
Christian	Spiritually challenged
Angelic intervention	Coincidence
Blind	Visually impaired
Deaf	Hearing impaired
Homosexual	Gay, gender oriented

Midgets	Vertically challenged
Liar	Verbally challenged
Brat	Dysfunctional child
Lazy	Horizontally challenged
Junkie	Drug dependency
Murder by doctor	Euthanasia
Murder by doctor	Abortion
Pro-life	Pro-choice
Stupid	Educationally challenged
Starving	Sustenance deprived
Handicapped	Physically impaired
Ugly	Physically challenged
Ugly	Great conversationalist
Ugly	Wonderful companion
Criminals	Inmates or freedom challenged
Terrorists	Insurgents or freedom fighters

Attack on Republicans   Truth &
Conservatives

Attack on Democrats   Deceit and lies
& Liberals

Life , Liberty & the   Selfish concepts
Pursuit of Happiness   of life expectations

Constitutional precept   Separation of
of Russian   Church & State
Used in American Court System
To deny Christianity its voice
In the public domain.

The Church has tests of faith which is a test of qualifications bordering on perfection of character which constitutes in its perfection large bank accounts. Is this wimpy Christianity at its best? If not successful are we not Christians? Do we not bleed? Do we not weep? Do we not die like anyone else?

Do not doubt that the Lord is coming for only fools believe He is not. Do not doubt the sound of trumpets. You can say you are deaf to the trumpets, but they will sound anyway and those who believe will meet Christ in the air at the time of judgment.

How can any sane person think that dust we are and dust we shall be? Nothing before, nothing after? Why persevere to succeed if we cannot take it with us? Why do good if doing good results in bad things? Why make more judgments when it doesn't fulfill the base desire of the heart and that is to sin with reveling in that sin? Why do we feel empty when God is explained away and rejected? We know there is life inside us and that life is a soul given to us to be cherished as a temple. Why is there guilt if the spiritual realm does not exist? Do we innately know right from wrong through an evolutionary process of rebirth? Does some part of us become our children where good and poor judgments are biologically added to the generic mix of our sons and daughters? Why should we feel guilty for our sins even when no one is watching? In a wimpy Christian society how can anyone deny the resurrection of Jesus the Christ, yes Jesus the Christ. We spend so much time giving Jesus the last surname of Christ as if we are speaking of the family of Christ. It is a small point, but in the age we live in it is important to know that Jesus is our Savior, the Son of God, and the Christ who offers eternal life. God does not glibly say to us if you follow my rules you will receive a key to the kingdom and if you do not follow Me, I'll give the key to someone else. God is not an owner of a frat house, but heavenly mansions.

In wimpy Christianity who would sacrifice their lives and souls based upon a lie? Why is there such hatred for Christianity except out of guilt and fear that makes us uncomfortable? The truth is simple, yet the ramifications are profound. If you accept the realization of the Resurrection you accept the foundation of Christianity. If accept the Resurrection you are the enemy of unbelievers for being a threat to their lifestyle. If you accept the Resurrection you have given up this life to justify and satisfy God's purpose in your life. If you accept the

Resurrection the gates of Heaven are open, the throne of God is within your view and the embrace of the Holy Spirit is everlasting. If you accept the Resurrection ridicule and persecution will follow through innuendo, insults, shunning and in many countries imprisonment and death.

Wimpy Christianity does not want to have enemies and so having the strength to say this is abusive, illogical and politically incorrect. Putting your life on the line can only happen if you are certain of that Resurrection. Wimpy Christianity calls Jesus "The human one" Angels are only "messengers" and Christ is the "anointed one". Why disguise the truth with a new reality? How much change is acceptable? Those who reject Jesus as the Son of God will not change their minds no matter the cloak and dagger language of a new Bible being written. Wimpy Christianity no longer sees things in black or white for fear of a backlash. Thousands of Christians are dying in Africa because they stand for what they believe unto death.

Wimpy Christianity make movies that questions that our decisions will send us to heaven or hell. Wimpy Christianity questions a God that sends those who reject Him to an eternal death. If you know the consequences of your actions and reject

Christ, yet believe that you will still go to heaven constitutes Christian anarchy. There is a hell and the following verses prove it.

"You snakes! You brood of vipers! How will you escape
    being condemned to hell?"
Matthew 23:33

"The rich man also died and was buried. In hell where he was
in torment, he looked up and saw Abraham far away with Lazarus by his side. So he called to him "Father Abraham, have pity on me and send Lazarus to dip the tip of his finger
in water and cool my tongue, because I am in agony in this fire."
Luke 16: 22-24

"Do not be afraid of those who kill the body but cannot kill the
soul. Rather, be afraid of the one who can destroy both soul and body I hell."
Matthew 10:28

CHAPTER NINETEEN
So she's naked,
Perversion,
Is a Constitutional right

In the dark realm of the senses there is no room for God. It tends to dull the sensual experience if God is looking over one's bare shoulder. God brings guilt into the guilty experience. The dilemma is how to experience the seven deadly sins without them being deadly. We are the last bastion that holds moral strength and righteousness in our grasp. To let it go would destroy us all.

Raindrop evaporation theory is a popular belief of many individuals. Individuals who say that as long as you acknowledge God in some form and lead a productive life, you will be rewarded with a free pass to heaven. It is the same as a raindrop that falls to the ground and after the sun comes out will evaporate toward heaven. So goes the theory that anyone who dies, their soul will evaporate and go to heaven. This ignores John 3:16. It would be nice and gracious to have God allow the famous writers, politicians, comedians and actors entertaining angels. That is not the purpose of heaven. Heaven is where God is glorified in His works, not ours.

There is no power in the Spirit without knowledge of the scriptures. There is no power of the Spirit without the wisdom of scripture. There is no power with the Spirit if there is no acceptance of the scriptures. There is no power for the Spirit without Christ in the scriptures.

Church is no social function, but a fellowship of believers with one purpose and that is to honor God. God does not want tithes if only for tax purposes. God does not prayer if it is wordless meanderings. God does not want converts if they are spiritless zombies. God knows the true and loyal heart which cannot be hidden from Him.

So how do we bring the issue of pornography with the above subject of the church? The fixation of pornography is the fantasy of presumed pleasure that something else is more fulfilling than your own relationship. We assume the best of a guilty imagination. We look for imaginative excuses are safe for us and detrimental to others for fulfillment. We, ourselves, might not want to suffer the indignity of the aberration but we perceive a healthy excitement in viewing it.

Like any other vice it becomes a addiction. All consuming and destructive to the spirit. It always spirals downward into a pit that is worse than the opening around it.

The spirit within oneself tells you it is unhealthy until deaf ears ignore the guilt and warnings. Like a drug it is easier to give in and enjoy the momentary indulgence no matter the cost of the embarrassment of exposure.

Pornography is a world of sexual illusion where the act can rarely be duplicated with the same emotional and seemingly fulfilling impact in reality. It is the lie of sexual fantasy that the visual orgasm is superior to a mundane marital one. It is the death of many marriages that wives or husbands see these adult stars perform sex at any time and any place with the same enthusiasm night or day. In the real world marriage is more than sexual Olympics where one partner needs to suffer through intimate debasement to be happy. It skews God's plan for sexual fulfillment in a marriage where one partner is subjected to an intense push to be objects of desire than a life partner making family decision and intimacy is not based on sex.

Should we pass more laws to suppress pornography? How long before the same laws are used against Christianity when those in power believe our faith is a crime against the moral base of our nation? Many great nations have fallen from political corruption and sexual deviant appetites.

On TV a glimpse of nakedness was all right until the glimpse became a glance into a loving momentary embrace of the eyes, then a short scene of lovers to a kiss between two women to a kiss between two men in a gratuitous love scene.

Then we have strippers wrapping themselves around poles to sexual sighs and heaves until the change to light bondage, rape and open homosexuality. It always starts innocently with the question 'How bad a prude are you for one little kiss?' or 'How much of a prude are you for the naked backside of a man or woman?' 'Isn't the naked body beautiful?' 'Do you not see the backsides of babies in commercials?' 'Did not God make His creatures naked in Genesis and did He not give us the urge to do what we now say is sinful?' 'Isn't sex a wonderful gift?' Isn't beautiful to see two women kissing?' 'Aren't all sexual acts a gift from God?' And the excuses and rationale continues forever.

Are we not made in God's image? If God made us as sexual creatures how can homosexuality be wrong? Doesn't the church have gay bishops? Gay pastors? Priests? Jesus never said anything against homosexuality or pornography so why all the fuss? Jesus did not outright condemn it.

When do excuses and rationalization stop? The backlash has been in place for some time with political correctness, censorship or lack thereof and separation of church and state that muzzle pastors, priests and rabbis from speaking out on various issues. To speak out against homosexuality is considered hate speech.

However homosexuality is not the problem because it is the sin we abhor not the individual until that individual demands the world change their lifestyle. When it becomes a political football and condemns Christianity there the problem becomes something we need to voice our displeasure against.

President Bush was asked if homosexuality was a sin from Diane Sawyer on Dec. 16th, 2003 and his answer was "We are all sinners." It is true we are all sinners, yet those sins condemn us if we do not ask for forgiveness. No matter the sin, without repentance and forgiveness. What awaits us is a dark journey into the vacuum of Hell. A place apart from God with perhaps a lake of fire, eternal darkness or painful suffering in a locked room is not a willing option.

Knowing this we seemingly can't help ourselves in our degradation. We like our sins. We keep them as pets stroking and feeding them, hearing them purr, enjoying the satisfaction of their taste and sound. There is no leash when our sins want to play, take a walk or whisper in our ears they are the masters and not us.

First amendment, first amendment, first amendment. In a free society the first amendment in regards to pornography must be allowed. Only those who want it abolished should not be silent to invoke their right to speak against it. Pornography is an image that can never be erased from the mind. It gives rise to the fantasy of the ultimate orgasm, the ideal copulation that is not found except in the institution of marriage. In fact, love has nothing to do with sex according to these fantasies. It is a purely selfish act with no feeling afterward except to search for the next conquest.

Women are the to suffer in this industry because they are abused by both men and women. In fact, women abuse themselves more thoroughly than any man could. Yet, where is the outrage from women's groups? That outrage seems to be reserved for abortion, government and business. That is not to say government and business are areas women should not have a voice in, but there are thousands of women who abuse themselves and each other for thirty pieces of silver.

Men see these "perfect on-demand always orgasmic women" on film and they begin to judge their wives and girlfriends on that level. Soon the woman you love is no longer attractive, physically defective or sexually irrelevant. Images of sexually deviation call to destroy your relationships because you have seen how exciting it supposedly is. Love is not enough. Bonding becomes binding and reality becomes a yearning for fantasy. So should not the church speak against it?

CHAPTER TWENTY

I'm sorry The Constitution
Is unconstitutional

The Constitution is used like the Bible in different churches. It is taken out of context, interpreted to suit the needs of the powerful and few or a reference whose interpretation depends on the imagination or political needs of politicians and judges. We have factions that want churches off the air on Sunday, talk radio is radical right propaganda and must be suppressed. Condemned are public figures, federal judges and Presidents because of their faith in God. Somehow intelligence leaves an individual because he or she calls upon God for strength in making the right decisions.

Of course, it is better to enslave a nation in political correctness, our students with misinformation and tunnel vision while filling our government with those who view God as their enemy. Does anyone wonder why God is feared, why Christianity repelled from government, education and society in general? It is because God exists and they do not want to share their existence with Him. The reality of Jesus Christ terrifies those who refuse to believe and suffer greatly because they cannot constitutionally erase His name from our history.

To make decisions as our faith leads leaves us with little room for error. There is no edge, there is no game to play to make a few extra dollars, to have power over many or to thrust out our chests to show how important we think we are. The Constitution levels the field for all of us so why would we look to destroy it? Because of the Constitution we are the freest people in the world and now we endeavor to destroy that freedom? Are we insane?

Our forefathers were flawed men, but they knew without God they would fail. Our freedom is based on Christian men and women who fought for that liberty under God. Should we have followed France which fought for independence without God that brought Robespierre and the guillotine to power.

Some of the questions that come from this is when, to be President of the Unite States or a federal judge, being a conservative and/or a Christian make the candidate a myopic fool with the education of a slug and unable to read the Constitution much less interpret it? When does being President that claiming your faith makes you an uneducated buffoon? When, elected to Congress, to profess Christ you are an ultra right wing conservative dedicated to destroy this country?

So now we come to Separation of Church and State. How far do we go to keep the separation? How many laws were made from the commandment "Do not kill?" Do we rescind all laws pertaining to killing? "Do not steal." Do we rescind all laws pertaining to theft? "Do not commit adultery." Should we rescind all laws divorce laws that pertain to adultery? When we talk of a free society is it because we yearn for socialism?

Why is democracy a threat to our nation? Why does government have to control all aspects of our lives? Socialism imprisons a free people. Socialism is an abomination to a free people. It starts with the denial of the church and God. History shows this over and over again, yet we have powerful people yearning for it here. When one segment of society thrives on the failure of the other segment we have fear instead of hope, high taxation instead of investment and political gain no matter what the cost in freedom.

We are a weak nation when we refuse to sacrifice for others. We are an evil nation if we give up hope to other nations then leave them to their own destruction. Should we not speak of the evils of this world because we will be shouted down as intolerant? The world awaits our fall so will we be tolerant to the cries of unborn children? Should we be tolerant to the spread of AIDS by promiscuous sex and homosexuality? Are we intolerant by trying to save the institution of marriage which repopulates the rest of the world? Are we intolerant to stop the plague of drugs and alcohol? Are we intolerant to say the sanctity of life is for the unborn and elderly alike? Are we intolerant because we tell others that God will judge us for our sins?

Are we intolerant because we speak against mysticism and secularism which in o way leads to the kingdom of God? Are we intolerant because God rules our lives and we say we are not gods ourselves? Are we intolerant because we can prove through historical documents that we were founded as a Christian nation? Is that something to be ashamed about?

CHAPTER TWENTY - ONE
When is a church not a church?
When it is politically correct.

Churches are a place of worship. It is not a place for politics, issues of national importance such as abortion, pornography, euthanasia, taxes or anything causing controversy or grief for the government. It is a place of mundane scripture reading and lack of moral indignation towards the media. The church should not have its hand in courtrooms, schools, government, media or theater. Does this sound familiar?

The Supreme Court has stated that there is to be Separation of Church and State so that the mere mention of Jesus Christ constitutes ground for dismissal in schools and a red flag for those seeking office. School prayer was banned and Thursday moral instruction was excluded from school education.

The public thinks it is a plus to add gay pastors to show progressive behavior in the pulpit. The re-interpretation of the Bible believes tolerance for all sins will get everyone to heaven. How do we reconcile then the following verses:

"You are the salt of the earth, But if the Salt loses its flavor, how

Can It be made Salty again? It is no longer
Good for anything, except to be
Thrown out and trampled by men."

Matthew 5:13

The church must stand and speak:

For	Against
Christ	Humanism
Life	Abortion
Dignity in death	Euthanasia
Freedom	Government control of all things
Free Enterprise	Socialism (Progressivism)
Equality	Hyphenated Legislation
Marriage	Gay Libertarianism & divorce on demand
Abstinence	Premarital sex
Biblical morality	Psychological morality
Life everlasting	Dust to dust eat, drink & be merry
Creation	Evolution
Law and order	Chaos
Prayer in Schools	Atheism in school
Factual education	Political correctness, socialized instruction, & revisionist history
Patriotism	Selfish disfranchisement

If Christianity is the worst for this country why are we not Muslim? Why not Zoroastrians? Buddhists? Why is the Dali Llama not our President? Is it all an accident? Why did the Pilgrims end up at Plymouth instead of the lower east coast where they expected?

What is the church experience for a congregation? A social event not to be confused with giving our time and devotion to God? A time of penance, freeing us from guilt that we sat through an hour of religious gesturing and posturing? A time of tax deduction? False piety? Pharisaical bombast? The church is all around us and within us. It is not a natural state of mind, but a supernatural one. We need to be super achievers of the faith through humbleness without being abused, happiness of spirit without joyful insanity, direction without blinders and a sense of purpose without fanaticism.

Martyrdom is not a gift of the Spirit if death is what we are seeking. Martyrdom comes willingly in an unwilling situation not by choice, but by truth of circumstances. "Here I stand, I can do no other." Rings true as Martin Luther standing before his peers could not deny the truth. What price is martyrdom if it is only to glorify yourself? The difference between martyrdom and suicide is the situation between the glorification of Christ and the glorification of the act itself. To die is easy, but to want to live yet die for Christ is not easy.

How many are willing to die for our basic freedoms and vote for those who look for the good of everyone other than themselves? Fortunately our country has not come to a civil war for our freedoms, but we are on the threshold of that change if we stay silent.

We cannot allow others to dictate our conscious about political activism, voting or speaking against the evils that now are being accepted in our society. We do not choose violence to stop abortion, we are tolerant to homosexuality without acceptance we respect the elderly and not threaten them with euthanasia as a reward for their long life and experience. We do not accept socialism as the future course of our country because socialism leads to slavery.

Where do our freedoms go if socialism succeeds? To South America? Africa? Europe? Our greatest enemy is tolerance for it has destroyed empires. We turn from God and God will turn from us. The Roman
Empire destroyed itself with complacency, tolerance and corruption. Russia could not sustain socio-communism because all people

year to be free. History is littered with past empires, but many in this country seek to perfect imperfection. Socialism does not work for it pushed aside our faith and our church.

It is difficult to be fair in a society where someone feels slighted or abused in every decision that is made. Decisions are to be made for the majority not the minority. The problem is that the courts are filled with lawsuits for purported hate crimes, hate speech, prayer in schools, prayer at ball games, the Ten Commandments, the teaching of the Bible in schools etc. Saying the Lord's Prayer is not hate speech, but a symbol of hope.

Should we not speak of the evils of this world because we will be shouted down as intolerant? Are we intolerant to say the sanctity of life is for the unborn and elderly alike? Are we intolerant because we want to stop the spread of A.I.D.S.? Are we intolerant to stop the plague of alcoholism and drugs? Are we intolerant because we tell others that God will judge us for our sins? Are we intolerant because we speak against mysticism and secularism which is in no way leads to the Kingdom of Heaven? Are we intolerant because God rules our lives and we say we are not gods ourselves? Are we intolerant because we can prove through historical documents that we were founded as a Christian nation? Is that something to be ashamed about?

Why is there such a litany of hate at the mention of Jesus Christ unless He is such a threat to the haters of this way of life. Such guilt must cry out against God or it would have to acknowledge what they do is wrong. This guilt would destroy the lives of the supposed righteous that cling to the tyranny of secularism. The guilty would rather suffer in their guilt than be healed from it. The guilty would kill the truth to stay right in their opinions.

In the dark realm of the senses there is no room for God. It tends to dull the sensual experience if God is looking over one's shoulder. God brings guilt into the guilty experiences of life. The dilemma is how to experience the seven deadly sins without them being deadly.

We curse God and the man who says a loved one has not gone to heaven because they were faithless. We hear "But he/she gave millions to the poor, to charities and foundations?" or "He/she loved their spouse all their lives."

"Not everyone who says to me, 'Lord, Lord,' will enter the Kingdom of Heaven,

But only he who does the will of my Father
        Who is in Heaven. Many will say to
Me on that day, 'Lord, Lord, did we not
        Prophesy in Your name, and in Your
Name drive out demons and perform many
        Miracles? Then I will tell them
Plainly: 'I never knew you. Away from me
        You evildoers!"
                                            Matthew 7: 21-23

Good people do not go to Heaven
because they were good. "I am the Way…"
Famous individuals do not see God because
they were famous being themselves. "I am
the Truth…." Relatives do not go to Heaven
because we wish it so. "I am the Life…"
This is not cruel, but realistic in the reading
of Scripture because Jesus said: "No one
comes to the Father except through Me."
John 14:6.
        In my own life this true for I have had
to come to grips with the deaths of my
father, mother and older brother who refused
to accept Christ as their Savior because they
could not believe they could be forgiven. I
have a younger brother in prison who caused
the deaths of my mother and older brother
whom I write about the forgiving nature of
God. He has found Christ in the Catholic
Church and I believe will be redeemed in the
future. Trying to understand this is not an

easy task, but it is one Christ has given me. Forgetting the past eases the memory of what could have been. For some the past is always present, hard to lose as a shadow following your footsteps. How can one erase the vision of a mother stabbed to death and tossed into a filthy old shower stall covered in blankets? How can one erase a vision of a brother's head shot off with a shotgun and know who the one who did it is your younger brother? I wake up in a sweat sometimes seeing these images and yet I write to my brother and forgive him as God has forgiven him.

As Christians we should say I do not have the light, or the word or the life. The Lord our God has all that. Do not look to me for perfection and glory for it will not be found in me. I seek the same things you do. Sometimes a glimmer comes from what you might see in me, but it is not mine, but His. There is always hope and dreams to come , but we doubt and hesitate because we are never sure. Yet this is our human side that fights the Spirit that tells us the hopes and dreams are true.

As Christians, in the worst of times we thank God for bringing us through them. It is our nature not to turn our back on God, but ourselves. We expect to fail because we are weak and we hope the strong hand of

God will lift us up again. That is a false assumption for if we truly have God in our lives we would expect to stand strong in the worst of times. Our lives are His.

We are only one person, what can one person do? How can one person change the world? Mother Theresa. How can one person reach the rest of the world? Billy Graham. How can one person involve himself with the legal system to protect all Christians? Dr. James Kennedy. How could one person proclaim the word of God to all? Dr. James Dobson. The list is long and distinguished.

When do excuses and rationalization stop? The backlash has been in place for some time with political correctness, censorship and separation of Church and State that muzzle pastors, priests and rabbis from speaking out on various issues. The church is told that it cannot be political or involve itself with social issues. The Church is God's voice, not man's. The Bible is God's Word not man's. Who dares to speak for God if we say God does not speak for Himself? The answer is that the rocks will cry out and declare His name. Do we preach till we see the fog roll I behind the eyes of our congregations and then become silent? When speaking of common sense one must believe in right or wrong, things that are in black or white or we cannot judge what is right or wrong.

We cannot say 'I know this is wrong, but I will do it anyway.' Or 'O know this right, but I choose to do nothing at all.' Or 'I will do what I want because I can.' Everyone has moral judgment that turns off and on like a light switch. We all do it, some more than others. Some of us turn the switch off permanently.

So what is truth or absolute truth? Absolute truth defines right from wrong. It is the sovereign right of our Creator to judge us. It is the joy knowing the path we walk brings fulfillment of the spirit. It is our faith in Jesus Christ whom no other can contest without deceit, anger, false hope or threats.

What is an absolute truth? It is simply "I am the Way, the Truth and the Life..." All other truth can be compromised and set apart with gray areas and verbal shadows. Why seek absolute truth if you do not seek it absolutely? If you seek proof of God why would you deny the Word? We all seek higher truths that prove we are not living dust with finite memories.

Absolute truth uses no excuses, no apologies, for the rules are absolute and unchanging. God is not God if Heaven is compromised with human doubt. God is not God if His Word is deemed a lie. God is not

God if His people do not know Him, pray to Him and turn their back on Him. God is God whether you believe any of the above or not. There can be no fence sitting.

"These are the words of the Amen, the Faithful and true witness, the ruler of God's
Creation. I know your deeds, that you Are neither cold nor hot. I wish you were
Either one or the other! So, because You are lukewarm-neither hot nor cold- I am
About to spit you out of my mouth."
Revelation 3: 14-16

The Church needs address the mythology that has infiltrated our faith. We are told there are so many variations of heaven, hell, God and gods, life after death, ghosts and faiths. The truth is that there is a great chasm between heaven and hell with no way to the other side once one sets up residence in one or the other.

"So he (Lazarus) called to him, "Father Abraham
Have pity on me and send Lazarus to Dip the tip of his finger in water and cool
My tongue, because I am in agony in This fire. But Abraham replied, "Son
Remember that in your lifetime you Received your good things, while Lazarus

Received bad things, but now he is
Comforted and you are in agony. And
  Besides all this, between us and you a
Great chasm has been fixed; so that those
  Who want to go from here to you
Cannot, nor can anyone cross over from
  There to us."

Luke 16: 24-26

There is no purgatory, no second
chance after death and no reincarnation.
Prayers for the dead are useless so pray for
the living. There
are many things that happen in this world
which are incomprehensible and we ask
"Why me Lord?" His answer seems to be
"Mind your own business!" Why would He
sat such a thing? Is it because we are
unfaithful? Lack the will to understand? Do
we not see the big picture? We think we
know better, however:

  "For the message of the cross is
Foolishness to those who are perishing, but
  To us who are being saved it is the
Power of God. For it is written: 'I will
  Destroy the wisdom of the wise; the
Intelligence I will frustrate.'"

I Corinthians 1: 18-19

I have diabetes, high blood pressure,
Diverticulosis, Rheumatic heart,
Arthritis in my knees and back, high
cholesterol, scars from childhood acne and
boils. I consider myself a walking pestilence
at times. Tragedy in life? I have been
homeless in my early twenties without help
or consolation. My older brother and mother
were killed by a younger sibling who is
spending the rest of his life in prison. I have
been surrounded by attempted suicides
among relatives, alcoholism, manic
depression, bigotry, paranoia, pornographic
addiction, greed, hate and physical abuse.
What was there to show me that God is
good? How did I come to the Lord with such
chaos around me?

"This is righteousness from God
Comes through faith in Jesus Christ to all
        Who believe. There is no difference,
For all have sinned and fall short of the
        Glory of God, and are justified freely
By his grace through the redemption that
        Came by Jesus Christ."
                                        Romans 3: 22-24

Televangelists have fallen from
mighty religious perches so why would I
follow Christ?

"I am the Way, the Truth, and the Life.
No one comes to the Father except through
      Me."

                                    John 14:6

      I have been personally rejected in my
youth by my family, my church, my
community and my school. Why would I
forgive the rejection? Why would I care
about them?

      "For if you forgive men when they sin
Against you, your heavenly Father will also
      Forgive you. But if you do not forgive
Men their sins, your Father will not forgive
      Your sins."

                              Matthew 6: 14-15

      Do we try and act like men? Shall we
cry to our deaths while the Philistines dig
our graves? Shall we climb down into the
abyss and hand the shovel so they can cover
us up? Where are the men who speak of God
and raise the Word as sword against the
foolishness that now overtakes us?
      When do we say "enough!" How do
we know when it is time to listen to children
of lost bones and hear their cry? Is it enough
when prayer is silenced for Christians, but
not for other religions? Is it enough when
Christ is made the enemy and the Lord of

Hosts is blamed for suicide, murder, blasphemy and genocide?

We are no longer children of God, but His messengers, His soldiers of truth and His carriers of the Cross. It is manly to stand for Christ without excuses or regret. It is strength to quote scripture. It is glory to take abuse from the ignorant who live in their own deception within destruction. Why make concessions with lies if the truth is lost? Why make a truce when it only leads to defeat? Victory never comes from weakness.

Victory is not easy when the enemy mocks your fight.

CHAPTER TWENTY-TWO
It's not my fault
It's your fault.

Very interesting thing is happening with our President, Liberals, and the media. Our President says nothing is his fault, but blames Bush, Europe, the Tea Party, Republicans, the weather, sunspots and anyone and everything that moves. No responsibility whatsoever, no sense of history, and no actual facts.

Short history lessons:
1) Lincoln, a republican freed the slaves.
2) Southern Democrats established the KKK
3) Federal taxes came from Franklin Delano Roosevelt.
4) LBJ started expansion of the Welfare State putting Afro-Americans under financial slavery.
5) Raising taxes in all areas come from Democrats.
6) Republicans helped give right to vote to Afro-Americans

The list is longer, but what does it matter since the blinders are on and revision history only destroys Washington, Jefferson and other forefathers pointing out they were slave holders instead of praising the liberation of our country from tyranny. Even today when our past heroes are mentioned there is always a "but..." But they were slave owners, but they were deists not Christians, but they believed in Separation of Church and State, but the Constitution they wrote is an archaic piece of paper, but they had different moral values and intolerant with views other than their own. When this country succeeded in greatness we hear that it was a "white nation" where only one race enjoyed that greatness.

Hmmmm, let's see:

1) Booker T. Washington- Educator
2) Thurgood Marshall- Lawyer-Supreme Court Justice
3) Louis Armstrong- Jazz
4) Oprah Winfrey
5) Tiger Woods
6) Chuck Berry
7) Bill Cosby
8) Michael Jordan
9) Barak Obama
10) Lonnie Johnson-Engineer
11) Percy Julian- Medicine
12) Granville Woods- Inventor
13) Duke Kahanamoku- Surfing
14) Dr. Feng Shan- Hero WWII
15) Dalip Singh Saund- First Asian in Congress

16)Steven Chu- Physics
17)Yo-Yo Ma- Music
18)Maya Lin- Architecture
19)Amy Tan- Writer.

I found these people with little trouble on the Inter-Net. All nationalities have the opportunity to succeed in America because we are all Americans with the same opportunities. Most of the famous individuals in our history was because the nation was dominated by white immigrants.

CHAPTER TWENTY-THREE

Hope & Change, whereas I have hope
I will find change in my pocket where
Dollar bills used to be.

Capitalism versus Socialism, what's the difference? Socialism has been proven to be a gateway to instant poverty. Yes, everyone is the same while a few are in charge and very wealthy. The ones who are the same are dependent on the government using limited entitlements to reinforce that dependency. Capitalism is the ability to choose to work hard to become wealthy with that hard work without government interference. Everyone has the chance to be wealthy in a Capitalist society where Free Enterprise works the best no matter what socialists tell you.

Now this leads us to the fact that the Constitution says we are a Republic in Article IV section 4 which states "The United States shall guarantee to every State in this Union a Republican form of government and shall protect each of them against invasion."

The difference between a Republic and a Democracy? A Republic is based on Judeo-Christian ethics and morals whereas a Democracy where the people vote whatever fancies their tastes can vote to have murder legal, rape legal or whatever they deem acceptable.

So what is next on the agenda? Is the slogan going to be "Damn the Rich!" Let's say it together! "Damn the rich!" Okay we take all their money and redistribute to everyone else and the rich are eradicated. Now the rich say "Damn the jobs!" Now you are out of work because you brought down the rich. What to do now? You rejoice to know the rich are no longer rich, but wonder what to do next. You can't run a business because the many regulations are overwhelming and the taxes if you make a profit are massive. If you do succeed and become rich yourself, we will have to bring you down for the same reason you started the whole mess.

If you survive the mess that wealth has brought you, you have to watch what you say for Freedom of Speech has, also, been taken away from you because you are rich. Not true? Ask Chick-fil-A CEO Dan Cathy who professed his faith in marriage between a man and a woman. The gay community doesn't like what he says so wants to destroy his company. Yes, this is socialism at its best working to deprive life, speech and profitability. Now add the Catholic Church whose beliefs are unacceptable when it comes to birth control.

Now add the infiltration of gay activists becoming Bishops in the Episcopal Church where one states that the "gay lifestyle is a gift from God." The church itself has become politically correct and undermining the moral and ethical authenticity of scripture. The church has no say in politics, you say. Tell that to Martin Luther, Martin Luther King Jr., Dr. James Kennedy, Focus on the Family and Jesus Himself. What about the American Revolution where pastors joined the military and spoke against King George the Third involving taxes and freedom.

This country was built on the freedom to choose our future not have it chosen for us by the Federal Government. In fact the role has been reversed since the Federal Government ignores the Constitution with the tenth amendment which states providing " that powers not granted to the federal government nor prohibited to the states by the constitution are reserved to the states or to the people."

Now what does that have to do with hope and change?

CONCLUSION

To recap for those who still may be fuzzy on the issues. Killing babies and the old folks is bad. Raising children in a moral family environment is good. Having respect and honoring our parents is good. Socialism leading to communism is bad. Capitalism which encourages individual achievement is good. Deleting God from every aspect of American life is bad. Encouraging a loving God to bless and protect us is good, but not a mandatory choice. Judeo-Christian morals and ethics are good. Anarchistic feel good hedonism is bad both medically and emotionally.

Strong families are good. No-fault divorce, premarital sex and sexually deviant multi-partnerships are bad. Euthanasia is bad, respect for the elderly is good. Laws for politically expediency bad, laws to strengthen the moral fabric of the nation is good.

This does not mean legislating morals, but upholding the moral respect for the individual. Favoring one religion over another is not constitutional. Respecting all religions that offer peace and mutual understanding is good. Religions that use religion to include the nuclear destruction and biological obliteration of other nations are bad.

The strength of faith is being able to stand your ground as the Spirit of God fills your heart with the truth. Those outside the faith who do not believe stand their ground even if it is quicksand and up to their necks. They refuse to move even if all is lost and the truth has overwhelmed them.

So when you pray to God stand your ground on His authority. When others tell you that you are intolerant when you speak against abortion, homosexuality, gay marriage and perverse theology stand your ground. When you are criticized for speaking against adultery and premarital sex stand your ground.

What stand should you make with these points? The act of homosexuality is the most selfish act one person can perform on another. It is a narcissistic orgasm where the male or female is essentially enjoying self-gratification from another. It brings on the destruction of marriage, family and moral objectiveness. It helped bring down the great empires of Rome and Greece which tells us why would not be immune to the same fate. This is not to say to start a war against the gay community, but to offer our love for them though disavowing their lifestyle.

We have become a narcissistic society looking only for self-fulfillment. Our churches are dying, the Spirit dims, the barbarians are at the pulpits and our schools while we swoon in our seats. The choirs sing as the congregation disintegrates into a sitcom or a Punch and Judy show.

We are told we cannot rely on God alone because He is just out or reach and faith is not good enough. We hear we have to "feel" God's presence and to that we must say "enough!" What cowards we are to allow the sheep to take charge of the shepherds. The four horsemen are coming and they wonder if you will stand your ground.

Our schools are teaching our children socialism which will be their future and responsibility. When did our Constitution become a safe haven for such perversity of our freedoms? Political hunger for passivism and tolerance so much so that another 9/11 would be inevitable. High profile senators speak weakness while our soldiers pay the price of those words. We no longer see traitors, but purveyors of free speech as long as that free speech speaks against war, cutting taxes and Republicans. There is no vision of the future only the blindness of the past. We stare so hard at where we've been that we have wandered off the road of where we should go. There is no forest now, only trees and we no longer can name them.

The only true hope we have is that God is in control and there is nothing that will change His plan. That is our future, our vision and our safety net. It does not mean we do not fight for what is right, but we make a stand that will honor God. Our battle is not with nations, but that spirit of darkness that so many seek and readily find. No one is immune, no one can escape the temptation, but we are justified by faith, not works. Our sins follow us, but God sweeps them away through His Son and our Savior, Jesus Christ. For this we do not apologize. For this we are not ashamed. For this we will triumph eve after the grave. As with Martin Luther "Here I stand, I can do no other."

www.ingramcontent.com/pod-product-compliance
Lightning Source LLC
Chambersburg PA
CBHW071040290526
45795CB00004B/1242